HAMLET

W0008077

TO BE OR NOT TO BE

Death Leaves Not Its Source

HAMLET

TO BE OR NOT TO BE
Death Leaves Not Its Source

Kenneth Wapnick, Ph.D.

Foundation for A Course in Miracles®

Foundation for A COURSE IN MIRACLES®
41397 Buecking Drive
Temecula, CA 92590
www.facim.org

Copyright 2004 by the
Foundation for A COURSE IN MIRACLES®

Printed in China

CONTENTS

INTRODUCTION[1]

The title of this book is taken from what is among the most well-known lines in all of literature, the opening of Hamlet's famous soliloquy: *"To be, or not to be: that is the question"* (III,i,56)[2]. The theme of the soliloquy is death, as it is of this book. As we will see in his speech,[3] Hamlet is caught up in the throes of the ego thought system. His ruminations about death are the ruminations of anyone who contemplates life, its ending, and all the problems that are part of living in this world. Those preoccupying concerns are exactly what the ego wishes for us as a distraction from the real problem, which is the problem of separation.

I shall begin by discussing the role death plays in the ego's strategy to keep intact its belief in separation. The concept of *opposites*, the principle that *ideas leave not their source*, and the idea of *death as punishment* will be the unifying framework for our discussion. This provides the foundation for my commentary on Hamlet's speech, followed by a consideration of some passages in the workbook and text that specifically address the idea that death is not of the body but a thought in the mind. Our discussion will conclude with a review of the portion of the pamphlet *The Song of Prayer* that describes death from the perspective of the healed mind. I will close with a reading of "Good Friday," one of Helen Schucman's poems.

---

1. A general introduction to this four-volume series on the great tragedies of Shakespeare appears in the Introduction in Volume I, *King Lear - Love and Be Silent.*
2. All Shakespeare quotations are from: *William Shakespeare • The Complete Works •* The Edition of the Shakespeare Head Press, Oxford (New York: Dorset Press, 1988). Line numbers cited refer to the first line quoted.
3. A copy of the soliloquy may be found in the Appendix.

Chapter 1

THE ROLE OF DEATH
IN THE EGO'S THOUGHT SYSTEM

For all of us who believe we are here in this world, the death of the body is obviously our central concern, both for ourselves as well as our loved ones. Freud said that "the aim of all life is death"[4]: from the moment we are born we are making preparations for death. All of life inevitably leads to dissolution or death, and this is a key part of the ego's strategy to keep us identified with its thought system. I will begin, then, by discussing the reason that, as authors of our own scripts and dreamers of the dream we call life, we write our stories with death as their most prominent element.

1. Opposites – One or the Other

First, and most significantly, the ego's thought system arises from death, which is the basis of Jesus saying that "death is the central dream from which all illusions stem" (M-27.1:1). The ego thought system, to state it quite baldly, begins with the belief that we destroyed God, and on His slain corpse erected our own selves: individual, separated, unique, autonomous, and special. Our individual existence, now thoroughly identified with the ego, thus began with death and indeed derives its very meaning from the thought that we acquired existence through the death and destruction of God.

Notice how the concept of opposites emerges right at the beginning of the ego thought system. It will remain its principal theme throughout, manifested in the contrast between two opposing thoughts: oneness and separation; and two opposite states: life and death. Death, now equated with God, is seen as the opposite of life, represented by our individual selves. The critical importance of this idea lies in the fact that it is the antithesis of reality, in which there are no opposites. Heaven, according to *A Course in Miracles*, is the state of perfect

---

4. *Beyond the Pleasure Principle*, SE-XVIII, p. 38.

Oneness; there is nothing that Oneness can be opposed to, and there is nothing that could be opposed to Oneness (T-18.VI.1:5-6). This is the essence of the Course's non-dualistic thought system. Thus if the ego, the thought system of separation with which we identify, is to survive, God cannot. Likewise, if God remains Himself, then a separated and individualized self cannot exist.

From the beginning, then, the ego set itself up in opposition to God, and the world it eventually made is by nature the realm of opposites, clearly evident in our everyday experience, where opposites prevail: good and evil, tall and short, warm and cold, north and south, male and female, winners and losers, victims and victimizers, waking or sleeping, life or death. Our world is predicated on opposites because our existence began with the thought of opposites. That thought then fosters oppositionalism, because it opposes the true oneness of reality. The mind of God's Son, from the moment he chose the thought system of the ego, essentially became a battleground of perpetual war with God. Paradoxically, he believed that God had been slain; yet he cannot help fearing that God cannot be permanently destroyed, and therefore he must continue the battle, lest he be overcome and slain by what must be a raging, wrath-filled God. In *our* minds—this has nothing to do with the Mind of God—there are two parties at war: God (the ego's god) and ourselves. One will survive and the other will die. It cannot be otherwise.

A world of opposites, however, cannot coexist with the world of oneness. A world of only good cannot exist where there is both good and evil. So when Jesus says in the text that we are "at home in God, dreaming of exile" (T-10.I.2:1), he is saying that being at home in God is the state of being awake, reminiscent of the famous story of Buddha, who was asked by some of his disciples: "Are you the great guru? Are you enlightened? Are you the Buddha?" He replied: "I am none of those things. I am awake." The true state of being awake is opposed to the state of being awake *and* sleeping, which is what life in the body amounts to. Another way to say this is that the world of duality or opposites stands in opposition to the world of non-duality, which is the state of perfect oneness.

The ego thought system of opposites can also be characterized as a thought system of *one or the other*. Someone wins, someone loses; someone lives, someone dies. Within the ego system it cannot be both. One cannot be both alive and dead. Furthermore, if I am to live, someone has to be sacrificed, the object of my specialness. If I am dead, then I have been sacrificed so that this same object could live. The ego's insane thought system gets played out in our minds as a battle between God and itself, the part of the mind that believes it is an individual self and likes being on its own. In the mind of the Son there is a conflict between this self that believes it is alive and God, Who the ego believes is hell-bent on taking back the life of separation it stole from Him. It cannot be too often emphasized that this has nothing at all to do with the true God, Who knows nothing about what has never happened in reality. The ego's god is simply the projection of its own insanity, elevated to the rank of the Godhead.

At this point, then, we see that the reason death is so central to our lives as bodies is that it gave rise to us, the ego's life that *is* the separation. God had to be sacrificed so that we could live—what the ego calls living—as separated, individual entities. This is why that line in the manual is so significant: "Death is the central dream from which all illusions stem" (M-27.1:1).

This same idea is discussed in the text in "The Choice for Completion," which poses the rhetorical question: "If you perceived the special relationship as a triumph over God, would you want it?" (T-16.V.10:1). Each time we indulge our specialness with either special love or special hate partners, we are re-enacting the ontological instant when we believed we triumphed over God. Extracting His strength, we made the ego self with which we all identify. Each and every aspect of the ego thought system stems from that prototypical act of cannibalism. What gets set into motion as an inevitable result is the ego's need to preserve this self, the individual life it believes it snatched from death and made its own: we live and God has ceased to exist, the victim of our perpetual war with our Creator and Source.

All this occurs in our minds, of course, which is why we speak of death as a *belief.* Death is not something that happens to the body, and certainly has never happened in reality. It is a *thought,* and since nothing just appears in our minds—we choose what we want to be there—there was a decision by the mind to have that thought. Once chosen, our experience is that the thought just happens to be there; but the ego originates with a *choice,* and choice implies at least two alternatives. Thus the ego's is not the only way of thinking, and from the very beginning there coexisted another Voice, with another thought system. This is the Holy Spirit, and His thought system is the Atonement.

The Thought of Life, being perfectly at one within itself, cannot of course have a Voice. Who would speak, and to whom? Yet, within our minds asleep, dreaming of separation, the thought of a separate Voice that speaks for our true state in Heaven is a necessity. We can thus think of the Holy Spirit as the memory of God that connects us back to the reality of Who we are as children of Life. Having fallen asleep, we took this memory with us into our dream, reminding us of the Source of life, *our* life. Within the thought system of life there is no possibility of there being an opposite to that life, no possibility of there being a thought of death. Once we change our minds to identify with the Holy Spirit and remember Who we are, the ego with its thought system of death is over.

This, then, becomes the crux of the problem. The ego fears that at some point we, as the Son, will recognize the enormous error of our choice—death over life, separation over oneness—and correct our mistaken choice by identifying with the thought of Life, the Holy Spirit's thought system of Atonement. Therefore, to ensure that we do not choose to accept the Atonement, the ego devises a strategy to have us vacate our minds. This next step in the ego's made-up thought system convinces the Son that he has sinned, not only by killing God, but by extracting life from His slain Self, as we have seen, so that the Son would have it and God would not. Overwhelmed with guilt about what he believes he has done, and believing the ego's mythology, the Son becomes terrified that somehow—magically—God will arise from His grave and come after him, seeking vengeance for what has been done to Him. What began as the seeming triumph of extracting life from the death of God now winds up as the mortal terror that this "life" will be taken back; that God will seize the life that was stolen from Him, leaving the Son as the slain and dying corpse.

Death, then, is the dominating thought of the ego's world—thought and body. Its centrality in the ego thought system becomes more and more evident as we look carefully at the world generated by the ego. The life of my self arose out of death, but if I am not careful that life will be snuffed out, just as within his dream the Son snuffed out God. Built into the ego's belief about life is that it is sustained only by extracting life from something else, which has to be killed so that we can continue to live. There is a striking passage from the manual, which I shall quote later, that is borrowed from an even more striking passage in *Hamlet* describing how life involves one thing eating something else, and then what eats in turn gets eaten. This ongoing pursuit of an object to be devoured is our "life." It is essential to the continuation of physical life that other life be destroyed; yet hardly anyone wants to look at the cannibalism of ego life that says we cannot continue to live unless we feed off something else, and when we feed off something else, that something else must die. Bodies have nutritional needs. Without eating they cannot survive, and this means that something must die in order for our bodies to live. This is the ego's law of nature.

2. Ideas Leave Not Their Source

Later we will look at a number of passages in *A Course in Miracles* where Jesus talks about death in the context of the principle that *ideas leave not their source*: Our belief in the death of the body has never left its source, which is the thought of death in the mind. The importance of that principle is that it tells us there is no world outside our minds. The idea of a physical world and a body that dies has never left its source, which is the mind that believes in separation and death. As we have seen, death becomes the food that nourishes life. It was the food that gave us life at the beginning when we believed we destroyed Heaven and killed God. It is the food that continually nourishes this illusion of physical life as we continue to re-enact that original moment when we sacrificed Another so we could exist. Thus was born the ego's world of opposites, and God became perceived as the enemy. We become preoc- cupied with food not only because of our need for physical nourish- ment, but because it is an important psychological form of nourishment as well, feeding our thought system of cannibalism and death.

All this is most unsavory; too awful to contemplate. Thus we try to cover it over. One of the purposes of the ego's thought system is to con- ceal the insidious nature of eating. This is not to say that you should not eat! I am simply saying that you should be aware of *why* your body has to eat, according to what *A Course in Miracles* teaches us about the nature of the ego. Our bodies have to feed off something else because *ideas leave not their source*, and the ultimate source of life within the dream is the belief that we fed off God, and continue to feed off Him. The content of the mind simply replicates itself: Love loves, creation creates; separation separates, cannibalism cannibalizes.

In the ego's insane world, when we stole God's power of Life we also stole His power to love, which is the power to create. This power to create has become grossly distorted in the ego's world, where it has become the ability to "miscreate," or to make illusions. The idea of death—stealing life from God—is the beginning of the ego thought system and its miscreated world. That is why the world is what it is. Despite all the pretty wrappings we put around it, this world is not a pretty place. One of the reasons the character of Hamlet has enjoyed such a fascinating appeal over the centuries is his pessimistic outlook on life. In his depression and misery, this melancholy Dane, as he has been called, expresses what everyone deep down feels about living as a body in this world. He speaks for the ego in all of us.

The foundation stone of the ego thought system, to say it one more time, is death. From that foundation arises the tri-partite constellation of sin, guilt, and fear, which results in the overwhelming fear of being punished and killed by an angry, vengeful God. This is expressed in a powerful passage in the manual: "An angry father pursues his guilty son. Kill or be killed..." (M-17.7:10-11). Death, then, is at the heart of the wrong mind, inextricably intertwined with the ego's aforementioned triumvirate. The ego's plan is to terrify us with its story so that we will seek to flee from the mind in order to escape the wrath of God. Following the ego's guidance, therefore, we project ourselves from the mind, thereby miscreating a body and world. The ego next seeks to perpetuate its illusory thought system by continuing to separate or fragment. Now the one Son, identified with the ego thought system and its concept of death, is fragmented into billions and billions of separate Sons, thoughts, and deaths. That process of fragmentation produces the physical universe.

Each of us, then, ends up in a body, haunted by the specter of death, which informs every aspect of our existence and becomes the motivating tension of our lives. We struggle to forestall the death the ego tells us is inevitable. Even though we sought to escape from the wrath of God in our minds by becoming mindless—making up a world and body—*ideas leave not their source.* The source of the idea of death and a vengeful God is always with us, but we no longer know its origin because we are not aware of the mind, and therefore do not realize that this mind has chosen a thought system of death. We just know that death and the struggle to survive, eking out whatever time we can, is what life is all about. That is why everyone is always at war with everyone else. Whether we do it as nation states that declare war on others, or as part of our everyday lives, we are all declaring war in one form or another. The *idea* of a battleground in our minds has never left its *source*, and so we continually battle an unseen enemy who we know in the end will inevitably destroy us.

That is the essence of specialness: dog-eat-dog; kill first before you are killed; eat first before you are eaten; seize what is yours before someone else does; and once you get it, make sure that you keep it. All this viciousness has its source in the origin of our individual existence, the root idea of which is: I exist because God was sacrificed; I have life because God's life has ceased as a result of my murderous thought. Such is the nature of our world, and why it is such a hopeless and depressing place, "a dry and dusty world, where starved and thirsty creatures come to die" (W-pII.13.5:1). When you look at the world with open eyes you realize its true nature. It is one of the purposes of *A Course in Miracles* to strip away the veil that conceals the thoughts beneath the surface of our ordinary awareness.

Freud was once taking a stroll through a lovely residential section of Vienna with his teen-age daughter Anna, and he said to her: "You see all those lovely facades? Things are not so lovely behind them." And then he added: "That's what it's like with people, too."[5] As Freud recognized, most of us have a seemingly lovely facade, but it is not very lovely once we look beneath it.

This also is what drove Hamlet—not insane, since he feigned his insanity—to despair. He well understood the duplicity of the world. He certainly understood what the body represented. But he, like Freud incidentally, did not know the way out. All of us find ourselves in a body, living in this world without hope, because everything here dies. Even what we believe has no life, like a piece of wood or a rock, will deteriorate and ultimately cease to exist. It may take millions of years, but everything that has form—whether we think it is animate or inanimate, alive or without life—will come to an end. This is poetically expressed in the following passage from "Forgiveness and the End of Time" in the text:

> What *seems* eternal all will have an end. The stars will disappear, and night and day will be no more. All things that come and go, the tides, the seasons and the lives of men; all things that change with time and bloom and fade will not return (T-29.VI.2:7-9).

5. *Anna Freud: A Biography*, Elizabeth Young-Bruehl (Summit Books, New York, 1988), p. 52.

This hopelessness is inevitable because death is the thought that gave rise to the illusion of a body in the first place, and *ideas leave not their source*. The idea of death remains in our minds, continually projected to be experienced in the body and its illusory world. This is the source of the pessimism found at the beginning of the manual, where Jesus speaks of the ego and its weary and hopeless world: "Time... winds on wearily, and the world is very tired now. It is old and worn and without hope" (M-1.4:4-5).

We thus find ourselves in a body, slaves to the thought system of sin, guilt, fear, and death as our irrevocable end. However, this thought system is no longer experienced in the mind, because we have forgotten our source. The ego's purpose for the body (which includes the brain) is to keep this source hidden, and what we experience as reality are only the shadows cast from within: the shadows of sin, guilt, fear, and death. Before the world was made—before the fragmentation of the Sonship—sin, guilt, and fear were thoughts in the mind. When the world came into projected existence, the ego's unholy trinity appeared to be in bodies. The ego would have us believe—in fact it has programmed our brains to believe—that sin and guilt exist in everyone else, but not in ourselves. Thus, we do not understand that the cause of our fear is the belief that we have sinned against God and deserve His punishment. Instead, we believe that our fear comes from *everyone else's sin*; even outside forces such as hurricanes, volcanos, bombs, or terminal diseases are psychologically seen as justified punishments for our sins. Anything except our own decision to be an ego is perceived to be the cause of our distress. This is another of the ego's paradoxes: we attribute our misery to something outside us, while also concluding that we deserve to suffer—the ego will use any means to reinforce the "reality" of guilt.

The ultimate goal of the ego's strategy is therefore to keep us in a perpetual state of mindlessness, totally unaware of the problem's source. That is why the principle *ideas leave not their source* is so important, and why Jesus refers to it so often throughout *A Course in Miracles*. It is what helps us understand that what we perceive outside is nothing more than the projection of a thought we have chosen inside. The world we perceive has never left its source in the mind, which is another way of saying there is no world "out there." It is just a dream. When we awaken from the dream of separation and individuality, the world will disappear, just as when we are asleep at night having a dream, we do not realize its unreality until we awaken. Then we realize we never left our beds nor interacted with other people; the dream existed only in our minds.

Jesus tells us that as we begin to awaken from the dream we call life, we will recognize that everything here is illusory. What convinces us—and what witnesses to the seeming reality of the dream—is the body, which tells us there is indeed a world, for we do not recognize that the body itself is part of the illusion. Reality is one colossal dream, but we think it is real and outside us because the ego has told us that ideas *do* leave their source, and have an existence beyond it. That belief began with the idea that a Thought of God could separate from His Mind. In truth the Son of God is forever an idea in the Mind of God, yet the ego has convinced us that that idea has now left the Mind. Separated from our Source, we enjoy an independent and autonomous existence.

The Holy Spirit's Atonement principle says just the opposite: *Ideas do **not** leave their source* (T-26.VII.4:7). Therefore, the idea of God's Son has never left, could never, and will never leave its source in God. That thought marks the end of the separation, which the ego desperately tries to forestall by keeping us from remembering our minds, so that we could never choose again. Since the thought of the Atonement—the Holy Spirit—exists only within, the ego seeks to distract us from our reality as mind by making up a world in which the body lives, governed by a brain and seemingly caused by biological factors such as genetic codes. Because of the ego's deceptions we have no clue as to its strategy, and remain mindless. What drives the ego's thought system is the core belief in death. Once we find ourselves in a body, death becomes the central problem with which we all have to deal, and our "lives" become desperate attempts to stave off the inevitable.

3. Death as Punishment

John O'Hara's first novel, written in 1934, was *Appointment in Samarra*. He introduced his book with a story retold by Somerset Maugham a year earlier about a man who encounters Death in the marketplace at Baghdad. He is so traumatized by the meeting that he attempts to avoid his fate by traveling to Samarra, about sixty miles north of the capital city on the Tigris river. However, Death already had an appointment with him *there*, and so was waiting for him on his arrival. The point of the story is that we are always, and unsuccessfully, trying to forestall the inevitability of death. Our efforts may be ingenious, but in the end our fate is sealed.

A similar theme appears in one of the finest films ever made: *The Seventh Seal* by the Swedish director Ingmar Bergman. It is a tale of a knight returning from the Crusades. On his way he encounters Death and, hoping to cheat him, strikes a deal with his Adversary. He bargains that if he defeats him in chess he will be spared. If he loses, Death can make his rightful claim. The game progresses well for the knight, and he has what he believes to be a wonderful strategy. They recess while the knight goes to church to confess, and while in the confessional he tells the priest he is playing chess with Death and reveals his plan, only to find to his horror that the priest is Death himself! His demise is now a foregone conclusion.

Everyone is trying to cheat death. As *A Course in Miracles* explains in this one passage, we attempt to beat God at His game, which to the ego is death: "You play the game of death, of being helpless, pitifully tied to dissolution in a world which shows no mercy to you" (W-pI.191.9:3). The true God's game, however, is Life; but, listening to the ego we think the game is to steal life, which then turns it into a game of death. The ego tells us we can beat God at His own game by seizing the life that is His. We naturally can do this only in the ego's nightmare of separation. But because we choose to listen to the ego, the dream now seems to be reality and we forget it is a dream, not to mention forgetting its origin in our minds.

In our delusional minds we truly believed we defeated God, and we now believe that we have become the author of life. We have become the creator and thus create ourselves. We are, as *A Course in Miracles* says, self-created rather than God-created (T-3.VII.4:6). After all, if God the Creator no longer exists, and we would have to come from some place or, better, from someone, then who better to be our creator than ourselves, especially since no one else is around!

We believe in our insanity we have usurped God's place on the throne of Life, and once that belief is set, the ego leads us to forget the true God, Whose memory is then buried in our right minds, covered over by the ego's thought system of sin and hate. This, too, is forgotten in our preoccupation with the projected world of sin, hate, and death that we have come to believe is reality. Once the ego strategy has convinced us that the world is in fact reality, we have to deal with the ego's version of God: a god of vengeance who sees sin as real, makes the theft of life real, and now has a plan to get it back from us—his vengeful plan of atonement. This necessitates lives of suffering and sacrifice, culminating in death. Early in the text Jesus says that sickness can be understood as a way of dealing with this punishing deity (T-5.V.5:4-9). Our choosing to get sick is a way of saying to our Creator: "You do not have to punish me. I will make myself sick and suffer, and that will be punishment enough." That is the bargain we strike with this insane god we insanely think is the true God. We somehow hope he will be satisfied with the suffering we offer up to him as sacrifice, so he will not kill us.

This is the delusional thinking underlying the insane traditional Christian view that salvation occurred through the crucifixion: Jesus' suffering and sacrifice. In this strange thought system a savior must suffer in order to satisfy God's bloodthirsty need for vengeance. Christians did not invent that way of thinking, though. It is found in the Suffering Servant Songs in the Book of Isaiah (42,49,50,52-53), which speak of one who is innocent and good—God's suffering servant— who sacrifices himself so that others will be forgiven. The early Christians took that idea and superimposed on it the figure of Jesus, but its archetypal theme—outside time and space—antedates history, being its true cause.

Now we can understand how all "people of the book" are insane. Jews, Christians, and Muslims alike believe in the same insane doctrines of salvation through sacrifice. Not only do we attempt to usurp God's function as Creator by stealing life from Him, we then attempt to usurp His imagined function as persecutor. The ego would have us believe that God's function is to destroy us. This deity is clearly the projected image of our own guilt: I did something terrible because I *am* something terrible; therefore I deserve to have something terrible done to me in return. My unforgiveable sin was selfishly to steal life from God, thereby murdering Him so I could live. Since I believe this sin is fact, I cannot but believe that I deserve to have the same fate befall me. Thus God becomes the agent of deserved retribution.

Again, we attempt to steal from God by cheating Him out of His vengeance. We try to make bargains with Him, as we shall see shortly. We try to keep death away as long as possible, all the time believing it is inevitable. But now, believing we have stolen the power of life from

God, we again seek to steal from Him what we imagine to be the power of death. Our life expectancy as a species—in what we think of as the civilized world—has increased. People now live longer and scientists are eagerly trying to extend our lives. All this is by way of cheating God. Now, I am not suggesting that we ought to die at the age of forty, or that early death is somehow more holy. But it is helpful to understand what makes our society tick. When we step back, using the perspective of *A Course in Miracles'* explanation of the underlying thought system of the ego, we can see much more clearly how our attempts to live longer are attempts to forestall death. All the while we are alive, believing in the inevitability of death, we want to pack as much as we possibly can into our little span of life—always trying to cheat God of what our egos tell us is His just due.

Suicide, the major theme of Hamlet's soliloquy, is a way of cheating God. It is another way of usurping God's function. At least if I kill myself I am in control of my fate. Our ego life is thus all about trying to cheat God and take from Him what we deeply believe is rightfully His—first His life, and then His justified plan of death. Listening to the ego we believe the reason we have life is that we stole it. The deep-seated guilt over that equally deep-seated sense of sin continually drives us to believe we are going to be punished. The triumvirate of sin, guilt, and fear becomes our reality, and thus we spend our lives trying to defend against the inevitable consequence—our death—of that "reality."

In summary, then, we are the ones who made up death, not God, because we are the ones who made up life—the ego's version of life. Once we believed in this thought, we made up sin, guilt, and fear. We next forgot we made it up, aware only of death's inevitability, without realizing that it is simply an idea that has never left its source in our minds. Now mindless, we have no recourse but to accept the inevitable, and then try to prevent its happening by somehow making a deal with God (Who we now believe is Death).

When societies and religions confronted this dreadful situation— the ego's "reality" of sin, guilt, and fear—they re-oriented their thinking: "If we cannot do anything about our physical death, maybe we can do something about what happens *after* we die." That is when the idea of an afterlife began to emerge. But even in the afterlife—since we are still thinking in terms of the ego thought system—there remains a state of opposites: Heaven and hell, winner and loser, vanquished and vanquisher, good and evil—the good thief who goes to Paradise with Jesus, and the bad one who will land in hell. At the beginning of the ego thought system God was good and we were evil: we stole from Him. We then quickly turned things around and God became evil— His weapon, death—and we the innocent victims of His vengeful wrath. Recall how at every level in the ego thought system there are opposites. It is not only that within the world itself there are opposites, the ever-changing cosmos itself is the opposite of the changeless Heaven. It follows, then, that in the afterlife we would find a world of opposites: reward and punishment; Heaven and hell.

Helen Schucman's sister-in-law, also named Helen incidentally, once told her: "I believe in hell because there has to be a place for the people I hate." When Helen told me this story, she made it very clear that her sister-in-law was not joking. This is a good example of why we need the concept of hell, a dwelling for the "evil ones" whom God will perceive as sinful. That is the context of the passage wherein Jesus tells us what we are essentially doing to our brother every time we con-sent to suffer pain or feel unfairly treated:

> You hold a picture of your crucifixion before his eyes, that he may see his sins are writ in Heaven in your blood and death, and go be-fore him, closing off the gate and damning him to hell (T-27.I.3:2).

In a world of opposites, a world of *one or the other*, if *you* go to hell I must go to Heaven. Maybe I cannot prevent God from destroying my body, but I can certainly fool Him into preserving my soul. This is why the doctrine of an afterlife holds such an important position in so many religions, both Eastern and Western. From the point of view of *A Course in Miracles* there is no afterlife, because there is no "life" to have an "after." Nothing happens when you die because nothing happens when you "live."

Everything in this world is part of the ego's strategy to make death real because, according to its thought system, death is what gave rise to life. When death is real in my perception, it proves that God has suc-ceeded in His punishment of me. From the ego's point of view this is a wonderful thing: if God has succeeded in punishing me it means I have indeed done something that warrants His wrath. Death, therefore, is the ultimate witness that proves everything in the ego thought system is true. That is why, when Jesus talks about death in the third obstacle to peace, he talks about it as the *attraction* of death, not the fear of it

(T-19.IV-C). It is that same understanding that leads him in the first two obstacles to peace to talk about the *attractions* of guilt and pain. As unpleasant as we might think all this is, the part of our minds identified with the ego is attracted to guilt, pain, suffering, and death, for they all prove that the world and body are real. The thought system that wants individuality to survive thus thrives on these attractions. To restate the point: Death proves there was life because I sinned against God. Otherwise why would He seek to kill me?

This universal ego myth finds consummate expression in the West in the biblical story of Adam and Eve. In the third chapter of Genesis we are told that God punished the two sinners by inflicting upon them a life of pain, suffering, and death. The reason that specific myth has held such a prominent place in Western culture for well over two millennia is that it contains the essential elements of the ego thought system we all share. That is why the Garden of Eden story begins the Bible, and its tale of sin and punishment becomes the driving theme throughout the Old and New Testaments. It speaks to that common thread in everyone: the thought system of sin, guilt, and fear, culminating in death. Again, death proves I have sinned, and thus truly exist as a separated individual. Above all, I have succeeded in getting God to pay attention to me. He is looking very carefully at what I have done, and does not like it. My ego loves it, however, because the fact that God is insane, vengeful, maniacal, and murderous proves once again that I pulled off the impossible: I actually stole life from God.

Among the meanest and most insulting things you can do to others is not pay attention to them. When people throw temper tantrums, for example, they demand attention. They do not want to be ignored. Indeed, the purpose in having a tantrum is to be noticed. Well, we threw one hell of a temper tantrum right at the beginning. And the true God paid no attention because He could not see what never happened. Therefore, we had to make up a God Who would pay attention, and it worked—at least in our delusional thinking. After all, we made Him up, and then told Him Who He was and what we had done to Him. The second and third laws of chaos in Chapter 23 in the text describe how God had to believe what the Son made of Him (T-23.II.4-6). He had to notice the fact that the Son sinned. Essentially, the Son told God: "You had better pay attention to me because look what I did, and I am still doing it."

What I want to keep secret from everyone, including myself, is that I like what God is going to do. I like the idea He is going to punish me and make me suffer. I like it because it means I won. I demanded God's attention and made Him as insane as I. Thus I do not mind having Him become the Creator of the universe. I do not mind giving Him all power in Heaven and earth. I do not mind giving Him power over my life, because once I have given Him this power I have triumphed, and will gladly suffer what Hamlet refers to as *"the slings and arrows of outrageous fortune"* (III,i,58). I will suffer happily because that is what proves I exist as a separate entity. And not only have I made God insane by having Him believe I sinned against Him, I have deceived and driven Him still further into insanity by having Him believe, in the end, that I am *not* the sinner; someone else is the guilty one.

We wrote our insane scripts—beginning with our families—so that we could have people we hold up to God as the sinners; the real evil doers, the wicked ones who deserve to be punished. If it is a world of *one or the other*—our way of thinking—then if God notices these others are evil He will punish them, not us. He may destroy our bodies, but He will take our souls with Him back to Heaven. At least that is what the ego tells us will happen. It does not tell us the truth, which, of course, is that the guilt we attempt to give away by projecting it onto others remains within our minds—*ideas leave not their source*—whether our bodies are "alive" or "dead."

Now we can see why we embark on these insane lives of special relationships where we love to hate, exploit, and cannibalize. We love to manipulate and seduce people into doing what we want. All this is reminiscent of the original moment when we seduced God into doing what we wanted. Once again, this is not about the real God and our relationship with Him, but about the God we made up and Whom we now venerate. This is the God that is worshipped in the world's formal religions, although we are really worshipping ourselves in the projected images of separation, sin, guilt, specialness, vengeance, and especially death.

And this leads us back to our friend Hamlet and his ruminations on mortality.

Chapter 2

"TO BE, OR NOT TO BE"

As we have seen, the rumination on death is the basis of Hamlet's soliloquy. I shall preface my commentary by summarizing the story of *Hamlet* to provide the setting for our discussion.

Hamlet's father—also named Hamlet—is killed by his brother Claudius. Within two months—in fact early in the play Hamlet says, *"nay, not so much, not two"* (I,ii,138)—Claudius marries Gertrude, Hamlet's mother and the king's widow. All this occurs before the play begins.

When the play opens, Hamlet's uncle Claudius is now king, Gertrude, his queen, and the thirty-year-old Hamlet has returned from the University of Wittenberg in Germany for the funeral. He sardonically mentions that he is also there for the wedding, which came hard upon the funeral. The ghost of Hamlet's father appears to his son and tells him what he unconsciously already knew: his father was murdered by Claudius. The ghost swears Hamlet to avenge his murder, and Hamlet's response to the vow of revenge he has taken on behalf of his dead father becomes the core of the drama.

What makes Hamlet such an appealing character is his obvious internal conflict. He cannot bring himself to kill Claudius, even though he is certainly capable of acting impulsively, as is evident on many occasions in the play. At one point, for example, thinking his uncle is hiding behind a curtain, he kills the concealed figure, only to discover it is Polonius, father of his beloved Ophelia. Hamlet succeeds in killing Claudius only at the end of the play, when he himself is already dying. But he vacillates throughout, and cannot bring himself to kill *"that incestuous, that adulterate beast."* Underlying all of this is Hamlet's profound pessimism, which I alluded to earlier. Hamlet hates the world and the body for what they are, and knows of no alternative way of perceiving them.

There are four great soliloquies in the play. *"To Be, or Not to Be"* is the third, and it comes near the beginning of the third act. Hamlet's first soliloquy appears in the first act (I,ii,129):

O, that this too too solid⁶ flesh would melt,
Thaw, and resolve itself into a dew!

Our prince expresses a desire for death and talks about suicide, but then says:

Or, that the Everlasting had not fixt
His canon 'gainst self-slaughter!

According to the Church, the everlasting God had ruled it a mortal sin to take one's own life, to commit self-slaughter. But in this third soliloquy, Hamlet is no longer even thinking of suicide as a sin. Now he contemplates the idea of death: *"To be, or not to be..."* means "To exist, or not to exist: that is the question."

What we learn from *A Course in Miracles* is that this is the wrong question. In fact, it is not a question at all but a statement. As Jesus says in "The Quiet Answer," such questions are really presentations of a point of view (T-27.IV). Indeed, there really are no true questions. What we think of as questions are but affirmations of the ego's position—the separation is real, as are all the components of its thought system of death. Most students of the Course would recall Jesus' answer to the most commonly asked question: "How did the ego happen?—"How did the impossible occur?" "To what did the impossible happen?" (C-in.4:3) It seems reasonable to ask how a part of God, a part of perfect Oneness, could separate from that Oneness. And Jesus explains in the clarification of terms that this is not an honest question. It is really a statement masquerading as a question. The statement says: "I believe the ego is real, and now I want you to explain to me how it happened." The question is thus a trick that attempts to trap the listener into agreeing with the assumption that the ego is real by having the listener explain how it occurred. Jesus' answer is that there is no true answer, only an experience (C-in.4:4). In the presence of love one knows that the separation could not have happened, so the question can no longer arise.

Therefore, Hamlet's assertion, *"To be, or not to be: that is the question,"* is a statement that says: "I believe life in the body is real," which means "I believe the thought system that gave rise to life in the body is real." Basically, Hamlet's question and dilemma are everyone's

---

6. The alternate reading of *sullied* works just as well.

question and dilemma. We are always asking questions about what we should do here. It may not always be as profound as: "Should I live or should I die?" but we all ask questions about what we think are important life problems: "Should I do A or B? Should I be with this person or not? Should I live here or there?" The minute we ask these questions we have made the ego real. This does not mean, incidentally, that we should not literally ask questions or seek answers to life's issues. The point is that our peace does not depend on the answer to the question or solution to the problem. Agonizing or obsessing over an issue merely reinforces the ego's plan of distracting us from the true issue— changing our inner teacher.

Notice, too, that these questions presuppose the reality of opposites. I can do either A or B, live or die, but I cannot do both. These questions make real in our minds a state of opposites, because they presuppose the reality of separation. The only real question I can ask is: "Do I look at this situation through the eyes of my ego or the eyes of the Holy Spirit?" Within the dream, the only true opposite is found in the contrast between the thought system of guilt, specialness, and hate, and the thought system of Atonement, love, and forgiveness. Everything else is a fragmentary shadow of the ego thought system of opposites.

Even though it would ruin Shakespeare's meter, Jesus would have Hamlet say: "To be, or not to be: that is *not* the question." However the question is answered, suffering is the result. "Do I continue to live and suffer, or do I die and suffer?" It is the same thing. As long as I maintain the reality of the ego thought system of separation from God— separation from the One Who is beyond all opposites—I will suffer, because the belief in separation itself harbors within it the seed of guilt that is the cause of all pain and suffering. If I believe I exist as an individual body, it must be because I stole life from God. That is my "original sin," which leads to the fear of punishment wherein God will rise up from His grave, pursuing me until He is able to take back the life I took from Him. This expectation is the source of all anxiety and fear. Indeed, *all* forms of fear are but fragmentary shadows of that original terror.

The problem is that we are not aware of any of this. As Jesus states in the text: "Of one thing you were sure: Of all the many causes you perceived as bringing pain and suffering to you, your guilt was not among them" (T-27.VII.7:4). We are not even aware that there is an ego thought system, at least not in the mind. We are certainly aware of people doing hateful things out of anger, but we usually do not identify that hatred as our own. It is everyone else's. Even if I admit: "Well, yes, maybe it is mine, too," still it is not my responsibility because the world made me this way. "Yes, maybe I am a monster, like everyone else, but I was made that way. I was not born a monster. I was born holy and innocent, but the world turned me into something else: my parents made me this way, genetic codes made me this way; there was nothing I could do about it." Hamlet himself gave words to this belief in his speech that scholars have used to develop their theory of Hamlet's "tragic flaw," the part of his character—as in any great tragic figure— that brings about the tragic end:

> So, oft it chances in particular men,
> That, for some vicious mole of nature in them,
> As, in their birth,–wherein they are not guilty,
> Since nature cannot choose his origin,–
> By the o'ergrowth of some complexion,
> Oft breaking down the pales and forts of reason;
> Or by some habit, that too much o'er-leavens
> The form of plausive manners;–that these men,–
> Carrying, I say, the stamp of one defect,
> Being nature's livery, or fortune's star,–
> Their virtues else–be they as pure as grace,
> As infinite as man may undergo–
> Shall in the general censure take corruption
> From that particular fault: the dram of eale
> Doth all the noble substance of a doubt
> To his own scandal.

(I,iv,23)

We are not aware of the real source of the ideas of life and death. In the ego's system, life and death are regarded as opposites, but in fact they are the same because the idea of opposites itself comes from the same source: the belief in separation. Everything perceived in the world is a projection of guilt, which comes from the belief in sin that says I have destroyed Heaven and placed myself on the throne of its opposite, the ego's thought system of separation.

Like the rest of us, poor Hamlet is stuck in a condition from which there is no escape. That is why he feels so hopeless and pessimistic. He is a thoughtful young man—he sees what goes on around him and he understands that people are not what they seem. He rants against

Ophelia at one point, saying: *"God has given you one face and you put on another"* (III,i,145). He sees that makeup is an attempt to hide what the body represents, and he despises it. This is not to say, by the way, that you should not use makeup. Whether you use it or not is irrelevant. We all put something on our bodies so that they will look better. We clean and dress our bodies; we attempt to disguise ourselves and hide. As Freud pointed out to his daughter, we seek to hide behind a lovely facade. Hamlet's problem was that he saw behind the facade, but did not realize that what lies behind is itself a facade that conceals the true loveliness of God. And so what he saw was greatly depressing, as he exclaims in his opening soliloquy:

> *O God! God!*
> *How weary, stale, flat, and unprofitable*
> *Seem to me all the uses of this world!*
> *Fie on 't! o fie! 'tis an unweeded garden,*
> *That grows to seed; things rank and gross in nature*
> *Possess it merely.*

(I,ii,132)

We return to *"To be, or not to be: that is the question."* After his dramatic opening, Hamlet continues:

> *Whether 'tis nobler in the mind to suffer*
> *The slings and arrows of outrageous fortune,*
> *Or to take arms against a sea of troubles,*
> *And by opposing end them?*

He asks if it is more noble to struggle against what goes on in the world, or merely to let them be. However, everyone here struggles, for life itself is a struggle: Getting food is a struggle. Getting money to get the food is a struggle. Just living daily with our bodies is a struggle, especially as we grow older. Living with our psychological bodies is even more of a struggle. The self-hate and judgment we project onto others; our neediness—dealing with all this is a struggle. On the other hand, if we end the struggle and die, here is what happens:

> *To die,–to sleep,–*
> *No more; and by a sleep to say we end*
> *The heart-ache, and the thousand natural shocks*
> *That flesh is heir to, 'tis a consummation*
> *Devoutly to be wisht.*

This is the kind of thinking that Jesus addresses in the text: "There is a risk of thinking death is peace...." (T-27.VII.10:2). Life becomes so problematic, so difficult and painful, that it is rare that any person during his or her life has not contemplated suicide at one point or another as a way out, just as Hamlet is doing here when he thinks that it would be a blessing to die, to fall asleep permanently and end the heartache. To him that seems *"a consummation devoutly to be wisht."* This is what he believes he wants more than anything else. But then we discover another dimension to Hamlet's thinking:

> *To die,–to sleep;–*
> *To sleep! perchance to dream:*

He is talking about the dream after death.

> *ay, there's the rub;*
> *For in that sleep of death what dreams may come,*
> *When we have shuffled off this mortal coil,*
> *Must give us pause...*

Our guilt, which demands punishment, says that not only will God exact His punishment when He takes our physical life, but He will continue to punish us afterwards. These, then, are Hamlet's thoughts: When we die—which here is analogous to falling asleep permanently—what happens if we start to dream? *"What dreams may come?"*

Several years ago there was a movie starring Robin Williams called "What Dreams May Come," the title of course taken from Hamlet's soliloquy. The film told the story of a man and wife, whose children are killed in an accident. He dies, and later his wife commits suicide. The primary story has to do with what happens in the afterlife. The wife is consumed by guilt and hate, and is saved only by her husband's steadfast love for her. The movie borrowed not only its title but its basic theme from *Hamlet.* As our hero says, we do not know what will happen after death. And what gives Hamlet pause is his guilt.

As I said at the beginning, Hamlet is everyone. That is why his character has long fascinated us, why so many actors and actresses have longed to play him. Shakespeare's play expresses our universal emotions, offering dramatic insights into the horror of what it is to live in this body; even worse, it speaks to the idea that there is no way out.

As we have seen, and will continue to see, guilt is what motivates our lives and gives rise to these emotions. This will become even clearer as we proceed with the soliloquy. Again, Hamlet's guilt is everyone's; a guilt that demands punishment: "Even when I die, I will be punished." That is what gives pause to the idea of suicide. As terrible as it is to live in the world, the devil we know is better than the devil we do not know. At least we know the lay of the land here; we do not know what might happen later—*"What dreams may come."* We have a foreboding about those dreams because they are made from guilt's projections, leading to dreams of punishment. We see this displayed in artistic visions of hell, often painted in such incredibly powerful portraits, such as in Dante's *Divine Comedy.* Dante's view is summarized in the famous statement over the doorway to the Inferno: "Abandon hope, all ye who enter here."

All these expressions come from the projections of guilt that say: "I deserve to be punished." The first level of punishment is that I will suffer. Remember, life was purchased by God's suffering and death. That is why the mythology of Jesus arose and became so popular in the world. In that myth, God, in the form of the God-man, suffers and dies. Remember, too, it is Church dogma that Jesus is God; he has both human and divine natures. He has to suffer and die because of our sins. *A Course in Miracles* teaches our perceived sin is based on our belief we destroyed Heaven and stole life from our Creator. That is why every Christian who believes the Jesus myth must be riddled with guilt. The guilt over Jesus dying for our sins reinforces the underlying guilt we share because we believe we are responsible for his death. Indeed, many Christians were told as children it was their sins that put Jesus on the cross. The Course, from the perspective of the ego, reveals the secret thought that it was our sin that made God angry, vengeful, and demanding of sacrifice.

Why do people believe that? Because at the dream's beginning it was the sin of stealing life from God that caused Him to die. We know we did that because we exist. If we exist as separate individuals, God's perfect Oneness can no longer live. Oneness and separation cannot coexist, and in this sense we caused God to die. This is the basic archetype that is in everyone's mind. When people contemplate the phenomenon of Jesus, they can think of him only in terms of the thought system of guilt that lies buried in their own unconscious. They therefore project onto Jesus and God this idea that someone has to suffer so they can be saved. God had to suffer at the beginning so we could have life and be saved from the death of non-existence. We then replay that scenario in our religious beliefs. We believe we are saved because God suffers and dies. If you are a practicing Catholic, God (Jesus) suffers and dies everyday at mass. In the communion service the faithful consume His crucified body—the consecrated bread and wine—so that life arises anew in them. This strange ritual has had such widespread appeal over the centuries because it is based on the story of our guilt, and it reinforces that story in our minds.

Our first payment back to God for what we did is our suffering while we are alive, or think we are alive. The second installment comes when we physically die and God—the ego God—gets His retribution. He takes back the life we stole from Him, and we think: "Okay, God, you win; now, please leave me alone." But He does not leave us alone, because guilt is insatiable; it always demands punishment. Not only do we believe that God made us suffer while we were here (which of course is the suffering that we bring on ourselves), but we believe that He will pursue us in the afterlife where we will be condemned to hell or, at the very least, suffer in purgatory.

All this fear, guilt, and suffering is our own doing. We blame it on God, but we bring it on ourselves because we believe that it is what we deserve for what we think we have done. Every breath we take unconsciously reminds us of that original first "breath" we took as an ego, when we inhaled life and exhaled God. We consumed His life and discarded His waste. The body we made must likewise consume. We have to ingest life, and that is how we continue to maintain our selves. We inhale air and consume the oxygen, exhaling carbon dioxide. That is what we do with food as well: absorb the nutrition and excrete the waste. The body derives strength and continues to live at the expense of other life, which is a re-enactment of the ego's original sin when God had to die so we could live. Sin's certain companion is guilt: the overwhelming force that drives us not only to believe that in our death God has gotten His punishment, but that He will get us afterwards as well. It is guilt that made up hell, which is where everyone in this world believes they deserve to be.

As a defense, people cover their guilt and believe they will go to Heaven. They do not realize that simply by being here in this world, in a body, they are saying: "I deserve not only to be killed, but to be punished everlastingly." Guilt and its demand for punishment is *"the rub"*: the core of Hamlet's problem. To repeat:

> *For in that sleep of death what dreams may come,*
> *When we have shuffled off this mortal coil,*

When our body has died, what will follow

> *Must give us pause: there's the respect*
> *That makes calamity of so long life;*

Uncertainty about the afterlife, which is born of guilt, gives us pause and is the consideration that leads us to choose to stay here:

> *For who would bear the whips and scorns of time,*
> *The oppressor's wrong, the proud man's contumely,*

Contumely is the humiliating scorn that proud, arrogant people heap upon others. It is a form in which guilt is projected that then contributes to other people feeling more guilty and rotten about themselves.

> *The pangs of despised love,*

Here Hamlet observes what is discussed in *A Course in Miracles* under the topic of specialness: the pain of special love and hate.
He continues:

> *the law's delay,*
> *The insolence of office, and the spurns*
> *That patient merit of the unworthy takes,*

Although we may try to be good and helpful to people, in the end we will be punished, rejected, and unappreciated. In other words, nothing works in this world. So, why go to all the trouble of living responsibly and attempting to make a contribution

> *When he himself might his quietus make*
> *With a bare bodkin?*

Quietus is an Elizabethan term for "settling an account" or "discharging a debt." Here it refers to settling the account of one's life. One could put an end to one's life with a *"bare bodkin,"* which is any metal tool such as a sharp dagger or needle. I could so easily end my miserable life. Why don't I do it? Why endure all the horrors of living in this world when I could so easily put an end to it? I choose not to because I sense the voice of guilt, and fear what waits me on the other side. Thus do I keep trying to deny that voice by making something of my life here.

In 1973 Ernest Becker wrote a Pulitzer Prize-winning book entitled *The Denial of Death.* It is a wonderful book that from a psychoanalytic point of view describes how everyone in this world tries to deny death. Becker recognized that death is a central problem in our lives, but that we try to avoid it. From the perspective of *A Course in Miracles,* the book basically falls apart at the end because Becker does not have an answer. He concludes by saying that the best solution to the problem of death is religion, not because it is true, but because it works. Its dogmas and rituals allow people to deny their anxieties and concerns, spiritualizing them in concepts such as God's inherent goodness, an afterlife, and the magical belief that other sinners, *not themselves,* will pay God's demanding price. Nevertheless, Becker's is an excellent discussion that exposes our preoccupation with death, and how we all seek to deny it.

Not infrequently, people attempt to deny death by having children. They believe offspring will keep their lineage going. The thinking is that even when they die, there will be some part of them that lives on. The "great works" they do will survive and grant them immortality. They hope their children will live after them, carrying their memory forward so that their reputation—the heart of their identity—will remain alive. This is reminiscent of Shelley's famous poem "Ozymandias." Inspired by the life of the Egyptian Pharaoh Ramses, Shelley tells the tale of Ozymandias who thought himself to be great and mighty, a "king of kings." He built colossal monuments to himself, but over the ages they all were swallowed up by dust and sand, and were no longer seen.

In one way or another, we all attempt mightily to survive after death. To use a personal example: My father's side of the family is quite large in number. The children of my generation all have had daughters, and I remember at one gathering one of my cousins lamenting to me that this situation was terrible. It meant the family name would die out since there were no sons to carry it to the next generation. This serious concern is not uncommon. People want their name—symbol of their self—to live on after they are gone; just another way of hoping they can avoid death and cheat God. Everyone is in some fashion trying to do just that.

Now Hamlet continues:

> *who would fardels bear,*

Fardels is an Elizabethan term meaning "burdens": who would bear the burdens of life,

> *To grunt and sweat under a weary life,*
> *But that the dread of something after death,–*
> *The undiscover'd country, from whose bourn*
> *No traveller returns,–*

Bourn means "limit, boundary, or realm." So Hamlet believes that death is an undiscovered country, from whose realm no one returns, once they have crossed its border. He does not believe in reincarnation; no one comes back from death.

The dread of something unknown

> *puzzles the will,*
> *And makes us rather bear those ills we have*
> *Than fly to others that we know not of?*

Again, the devil I know is better than the devil I do not know. Hamlet senses the underlying guilt and sees that it is fear that keeps us here and has us choose to live. Hamlet's speech is everyone's speech. We attempt to prolong life as individuals, and we certainly do that as a society. Physicians and others are so desperate to prolong life that euthanasia is considered a crime in many states. In this country there is a widespread belief that it is a sin to take one's life, and even mercy killing is a sin because physical life is deemed sacred. However, we are really saying: "I want to keep life going as long as I can because I am terrified of what is around the corner":

> *Thus conscience does make cowards of us all…*

By *conscience* Hamlet means guilt. It is our guilt that makes cowards of us and forces us to stay here. We are afraid of the afterlife because of our underlying guilt.

As a quick aside, Freud was a lover of Shakespeare, and particularly loved *Hamlet*. In *The Interpretation of Dreams* he speculated in a footnote about what kept Hamlet from killing Claudius, the obvious action for him to take, given the circumstances. This is one of the intriguing problems of the play: What was it that prevented Hamlet from following his dead father's wishes and killing his uncle? Central to Freud's psychoanalytic theory is the Oedipus complex, which recognizes that each child secretly wishes to possess the love of the opposite-sex parent by eliminating the same-sex parent, seen as a competitive rival. According to Freud's theory this guilty desire lies buried in every human unconscious, often surfacing in the form of pathological symptoms unless it is somehow resolved.

Freud hypothesized therefore that it was Hamlet's Oedipus complex that impaired his ability to act. According to Freud's theory, the uncle did what Hamlet secretly wanted to do, and indeed, what every male child wants to do: kill the father in order to possess the mother for himself. There is enormous unconscious guilt about this parricidal wish. In Freud's view, it was the need to deny that wish, along with the associated guilt, that complicated Hamlet's motivations and interfered with his ability to act: killing Claudius meant killing himself for the same sin. Ernest Jones, one of Freud's most ardent followers, wrote a book entitled *Hamlet and Oedipus*, based on Freud's footnote.

Whether or not one subscribes to Freud's literal theory, in *content* he clearly recognized the powerful motivating force of guilt. We can see that the *content* of Freud's Oedipus complex is nothing more or less than our familiar Course friends, special love and special hate, which Jesus describes in excruciating detail. The central idea of the special relationship is that we wish to consume the object of our special love, cannibalizing it in order to fill what we believe we lack inside. Ultimately, we want to kill off everyone else, since we perceive everyone as a rival or potential rival. That dynamic of neediness, competition, murderousness, and guilt is the core of Freud's Oedipus complex, which we just discussed. Thus Freud believed that after three hundred years of people puzzling over the play, he had finally solved the problem of Hamlet's motivations and confusion. The line, "*Thus conscience does make cowards of us all*," tells us that Hamlet's guilt interfered with his ability to act, either to kill his uncle or himself. His guilt is our own, for we all harbor the guilt associated with specialness.

The germ of this specialness can be found in our original special relationship with God; our anger that He would not give us the specialness we demanded. He did not notice us, for He could not recognize our individual existence. In God's Mind there is no separation, so the existence of separate beings is an impossibility. Indeed, separation itself is impossible. Therefore, I as an ego do not exist. We hate God for that! As the Course says in one passage:

> You were at peace until you asked for special favor. And God did not give it for the request was alien to Him, and you could not ask this of a Father Who truly loved His Son. Therefore you made of Him an unloving father, demanding of Him what only such a father could give (T-13.III.10:2-4).

As God would not acknowledge our existence (remember that Jesus makes a distinction between the *being* of spirit and the *existence* of the ego—[T-4.III.3; T-4.VII.4:1-4]), we said to Him: "To hell with You; I will simply kill You off and make up a God Who *will* notice me." The God of the Bible is one form that special deity has taken; a God that most definitely notices us. In our insanity we do not care whether He notices us on His good or bad days. He could punish and even kill us, as long as He accepts our individual self as a reality; sinful or not is irrelevant to this basic ego purpose. Indeed, His punishing us demonstrates our power over Him: the power to make Him notice us so that our existence as individuals is validated.

Our guilt has driven us out of our minds—literally and figuratively —into a world in which we re-enact the ontological guilt over and over and over again. Without really understanding its metaphysical dimensions, that is what Freud observed and tried to explain. Our *original* Oedipal conflict is with God the Father. That is what crippled Hamlet and cripples all of us. It explains why we do not always do what we want, and why our lives so often seem to us as failures.

So Hamlet concludes:

> *Thus conscience does make cowards of us all;*
> *And thus the native hue of resolution*
> *Is sicklied o'er with the pale cast of thought;*
> *And enterprises of great pith and moment;*
> *With this regard, their currents turn awry,*
> *And lose the name of action.*

Hamlet is saying that because of his guilt, his resolve to fulfill his oath to avenge his dead father has been impaired. The natural resolve—*"the native hue of resolution"*—is obscured by *"the pale cast of thought.*" His ruminations, thinking and speculations, his musings about life and death—all stall his determination. This "*enterprise of great pith and moment,*" which he had sworn to undertake, he fails to complete, at least at this point in the drama.

In the midst of his confused thinking and doubt, Hamlet comes up with a plan, which is to have a play be staged which will re-enact his father's murder. This play-within-a-play idea actually precedes our soliloquy, and Hamlet's self-reflections—"*O, what a rogue and peasant slave am I!*" (II,ii,559)—is the source of another famous line: "*The play's the thing wherein I'll catch the conscience of the king*" (II,ii,605). Thus Hamlet arranges the play, hoping that Claudius will incriminate himself when he observes a re-enactment of his fratricidal act.

The basic idea here, again, is that because of his unrecognized guilt, Hamlet agonizes over his vow to avenge his father's death, stalling its execution. We are already in the third act of the five-act play. As further evidence of his discomfort and uncertainty, he dissimulates. He invents a plan to feign madness. (Some critics have believed that Hamlet was temporarily deranged—that he is not pretending—but that seems unlikely.) Yet all his thinking and plotting seem designed to keep him from acting, rather than bringing him closer to it.

Note that in this soliloquy Hamlet does not speak in the first person, as he does in his other ones. This suggests that Hamlet is speaking for all of us, not only for himself. We all share the guilt that confuses and disables our prince; the guilt that causes us to be afraid of what will happen after death. And so we choose to live and suffer here, seeking to continue physical life as a way of staving off the inevitable. Hamlet is saying, as we all say: "I at least know what I am getting here. It is not pleasant, but it is better than my fate when I die."

This reasoning from guilt, and the fear it inspires, explains why we all have come here in the first place. The ego told the Son: "If you stay in your mind you will be destroyed. Therefore, let us leave this mind and go into a world where we can safely and securely live in a body." Well, the ego lied! We are anything but safe and secure here! However, to give the devil its due, the ego did fulfill one part of its promise: by living in a state of separation we get to avoid responsibility for our choice, and have the opportunity to project our guilt onto others. Thus the ego told us: "Even though your body will be vulnerable and will die, you will be safe here because I will give you someone else to blame for the separation. That is why I have made you a brave, new world with all these people in it [to paraphrase Miranda's line from Shakespeare's *The Tempest* (V,i,183)]. You will thus have ample opportunity to project your secret sin and hidden hate onto them, causing them to be punished in the hereafter instead of you. You will be able to keep the separation—the life you stole from God—but someone else will be held responsible for it." This, then, was the ego's pitch to us, and we bought it hook, line, and sinker!

We are afraid of death because we think the body is a defense against the mind. We fear that when the body ceases to exist we will be thrown back into our minds, and that is where the ego's God of wrath will find us. This is the fear that Hamlet reflects in his soliloquy. We all live out of that fear, which is why we think physical life and our bodies are so important. We made bodies that have receptors of pleasure and pain so that our goals in life would be to maximize pleasure and minimize pain, prolonging life and avoiding death.

In the text sections "The Obstacles to Peace," we are taught that pleasure and pain are the *same*, because they both serve the purpose of making the body real, thereby making the ego thought system of specialness real (T-19.IV-A.17:10-12; IV-B.12-13). Therefore, our greatest pleasure in this world is to have pain, delighting in making someone else responsible for our suffering. In that way we believe that by being in a body we will escape the punishment of God.

Our problem, which Hamlet alludes to, is that the ego's strategy does not work. The real problem is in our minds, but the ego has us believe we have escaped the mind so that we would never truly look at its underlying thought system. Death, as we have seen, is an integral part of that thought system; a thought in our minds, not a phenomenon of the body. That is why Hamlet is asking the wrong question. The question is not about physical life and death: *"To be, or not to be."* That "question," as we have already seen, is a statement of our belief that the body and world are real. The real issue is that we are not physically here at all. Nothing happens to the body, because the body is nothing. Everything is a projection of a thought in our minds: the thought of life or the thought of death. The purpose of *A Course in Miracles* is to lead us away from bodily preoccupations, back to our minds where we can choose again.

A Right-Minded Hamlet

Before we move on to readings from *A Course in Miracles*, it might be interesting to speculate on what might have happened to Hamlet if, instead of listening to the voice of his father's ghost, he had listened to the Voice of the Holy Ghost (pardon the pun!).

For that to have occurred, Hamlet's guilt over special love and special hate—Freud's Oedipus complex—would have had to have been opened to re-examination. Therefore, before he would have acted at all, Hamlet would have recognized that what he was so angry about with his mother and Claudius was something he was secretly guilty about in himself. He would have asked the Holy Spirit for help, and thus would have realized—before he acted at all—that the drama he was seeing played out in the royal court was an outside picture of *his* inner drama. Assuming he was able to follow through on this process of forgiveness, he would have done whatever he felt guided to do by the Holy Spirit. It is quite possible that Hamlet would have been helped to see that his father's ghost was a projection of his own guilt, seeking vengeance for a sin that was not his own. It was thus his own ego telling him to seek punishment for his uncle rather than for himself. The Holy Spirit would have helped Hamlet realize that the vow he had made to his father's ghost was really an expression of the secret vow we all make to the ego's thought system of betrayal, guilt, and punishment by death.

Hamlet thus would have seen that his uncle was not an incestuous, adulterous beast, but a poor soul like everyone else, desperately trying to find happiness, believing in his insanity that it was in his best interests to kill his brother and marry his sister-in-law. Hamlet would have looked at his mother and seen another poor soul who believed in the scarcity principle—i.e., she lacked love—and so her ego left her no choice but to run into Claudius' arms. Our melancholy Dane would have looked with mercy on his family, rather than with judgment. Moreover, he would have felt compassion for Ophelia, rather than crucifying her. Her brother Laertes would be seen as his own brother, as beloved as was Horatio, Hamlet's closest friend. And he would have seen that his traitorous "friends" Rosencrantz and Guildenstern, acting as agents for the king in attempting to kill him, were but trying to survive, a survival that in their insanity meant killing off others.

In summary, under the Holy Spirit's guidance Hamlet would have looked at the special relationships in his life—all those onto whom he had been projecting—recognizing the insanity shared by all, including his own. Attacks would have been correctly perceived as expressions of fear, which were calls for the love—in all people—that had been denied. How Hamlet would have reacted on the level of behavior I do not know. But at this point in our revised drama it would not have mattered: he was no longer filled with thoughts of vengeance, guilt, and conflict. For example, he would not have said to his mother, "*I must be cruel, only to be kind*" (III,iv,179), which was the voice of his own guilty conscience, and which, in the play, necessitated the ghost's return to plead with his son to be merciful. Hamlet would have been truly kind. He might still have exposed the crime, but perhaps no one would have been killed, as in Shakespeare's play where almost everyone dies. Hamlet's actions would have reflected the content of correcting mistakes, rather than reinforcing sin.

The actual play ends with Fortinbras, Prince of Norway, successfully invading Denmark and taking over as king. Hamlet's father had won a battle against Fortinbras' father many years before, captured land, after which peace was established. But young Fortinbras now returns to take back the land rightfully belonging to his people. Perhaps Hamlet could have established Fortinbras king without having first to clean up the bloody corpses lying around the court. Perhaps the whole thing could have been resolved through forgiveness, without murder reinforcing guilt. Hamlet is the pivotal figure in the play. As his mother's favorite, and beloved by all in the court, he might have used his influence to bring about healing instead of vengeance. Unfortunately, this would have most likely made for a very dull play, but then forgiveness is much less exciting than revenge.

Now let us turn to *A Course in Miracles* and Jesus' specific teachings about death.

Chapter 3

DEATH ACCORDING TO *A COURSE IN MIRACLES*

"What Is Death?"

Beginning with the section "What Is Death?" in the teacher's manual (M-27), I would like now to discuss some of the passages in *A Course in Miracles* that specifically address the phenomenon of death. This will help us to see even more clearly how death is a thought in our minds, having nothing whatsoever to do with the body. The next section in the manual, "What Is Resurrection?" (M-28), reinforces this point in explaining that *resurrection* is the awakening from the dream of death. The body is not asleep; the body is not dead; and therefore the body does not have to be awakened or resurrected. It is the *mind* that sleeps and dreams of death. Everything occurs there. Thus death is, very simply, a thought in the mind; and resurrection, very simply, is the undoing of that thought through forgiveness.

The first sentence in this section is the one I cited at the beginning of Chapter 1:

(M-27.1:1) Death is the central dream from which all illusions stem.

We have already seen how that works: The ego thought system begins with death, the death of God.

(1:2-3) Is it not madness to think of life as being born, aging, losing vitality, and dying in the end? We have asked this question before, but now we need to consider it more carefully.

Jesus frequently refers us back to points he stated earlier, as he does here. At one point in the text he says: "Let reason take another step" (T-22.I.1:1), reason being right-minded thinking. He is saying here we are now going to look at this idea of death a little more carefully and deeply; we are ready to take another step.

In the second sentence Jesus is talking about the body: "Is it not insane to think of life, which we associate with the body, as being born, aging, losing vitality, and dying?" He is offering us the opportunity to understand and experience that real life is only of God, of spirit, and therefore does not change. Real life does not begin and it does not end. The workbook states: "We say 'God is,' and then we cease to speak" (W-pI.169.5:4). We can also state: "We say 'Life is,' and then we cease to speak." Life in Heaven is totally unknown to us, totally beyond anything we can comprehend, because we think life is what goes on here in the world, in our bodies. As Jesus explains in the text, we cannot even think of God without a body, or as having some form we recognize (T-18.VIII.1:7). We cannot help thinking of our Creator as separate, as being a person in some way, because that is how we see ourselves, and *projection makes perception* (T-21.in.1:1).

The idea that God and Life are pure *content* is at the heart of this discussion. When we think of the birth and death of the body, and the changes occurring between those two states, we always think in terms of *form*. The idea of form and the perception of change are inextricably related. Indeed, they are essentially the same. This is another of the ways in which Jesus helps us understand the difference between the thought systems of the ego and the Atonement. Our world of form, which arose from the ego, continually changes, like Heraclitus' river. Heaven, on the other hand, is changeless. Recall those beautiful sections in the text, "The Changeless Dwelling Place" (T-29.V) and "Changeless Reality" (T-30.VIII). We know God has absolutely nothing to do with this world, and *cannot* have anything to do with this world, because it is always changing. The idea of change has never left its source, which is the ego thought system in our minds; therefore everything here changes. The thought system of the ego began with the idea of changing the Oneness of Heaven, and all that seemed to follow but reflects that original change. In truth, however, nothing has ever changed *except* change.

Another way of saying that our existence as individuals began with death—the death of God—is to say that our lives began with change. Our individuality required the change of our status from a Child of God to a child of the ego; from a Child of Oneness and perfect Love to a child of separation and sin. That is the fundamental and only change. Since *ideas leave not their source*, the world directly mirrors the thoughts that are in the mind. Thus, in the second sentence here Jesus is telling us that because the body changes, we know it cannot be of God and cannot have life. The body can be only what Jesus describes elsewhere in *A Course in Miracles* as a parody or travesty of life, not life itself (T-24.VII.1:11; 10:9; T-29.VII.5:3; W-pI.95.2:1). He tells us in Chapter 23: "There is no life outside of Heaven" (T-23.II.19:1), a very strong statement that tells us that everything outside of Heaven is not life. It is not dead; it simply is not alive and does not exist. As Jesus teaches us later in the text: "What [the body] you have given 'life' is not alive, and symbolizes but your wish to be alive apart from life, alive in death, with death perceived as life, and living, death" (T-29.II.6:2).

(1:4) It is the one fixed, unchangeable belief of the world that all things in it are born only to die.

We discussed earlier that everything in this world changes; everything deteriorates, decomposes, and dies. Whether it happens in one minute, fifty years, eighty years, or a hundred million years, *everything* here will eventually cease to exist.

(1:5) This is regarded as "the way of nature," not to be raised to question, but to be accepted as the "natural" law of life.

That is how we all think, and it is important to acknowledge honestly that we *do* make this assumption. The fact that we might be dedicated and long-term students of *A Course in Miracles*, and understand that the world is an illusion does not prevent us from inwardly assuming and outwardly experiencing the exact opposite. We live our lives as human beings. Whether we like it or not, we live from day to day the same as people who have never read the Course. Even though we may believe everything the Course teaches us about the fundamental unreality of the world, our *experience* is just the opposite.

It may be very humbling to accept this about yourself, but it is quite important if you are to make progress with this Course. If you pay attention to how you live your life every day—even every moment—you must recognize this. We breathe, eat, recreate, and sleep. We do all kinds of things and may have varying levels of investment in what we do, but we obviously are all very much identified with our physical and psychological selves. Try not to make the mistake of spiritualizing your ego, or covering it with a spiritual veneer pretending you have accepted a holy identity, when you have not really accepted it at all.

(1:6) The cyclical, the changing and unsure; the undependable and the unsteady, waxing and waning in a certain way upon a certain path,—all this is taken as the Will of God.

The Bible has been so incredibly popular because it portrays God as the Creator of a world of change; and that seems to be the natural state of things. We experience change every moment of every day. Seasons change, bodies change, emotions change. Everything changes. How absurd, Jesus is pointing out to us, to associate such change with the Unchangeable!

(1:7) And no one asks if a benign Creator could will this.

The fundamental premise that you must accept as a student of this Course—otherwise *A Course in Miracles* is really not your path—is that God is totally beyond anything in this world. A non-dualistic Deity can have absolutely nothing to do with duality. Anything in this world must be the opposite of Him, and since "what is all-encompassing can have no opposite" (T-in.1:8) nothing here can be of God. Understanding this helps us to appreciate more fully the statement in the workbook that says: "The world was made as an attack on God" (W-pII.3.2:1). This does not mean that the world is a bad place, nor a sinful, wicked, or evil one. It simply does not exist, because an attack on God is impossible. It never happened and therefore is not reality. You will trip yourself up in understanding the meaning of forgiveness—let alone in its practice—if you do not accept this fundamental metaphysical teaching of the Course. It is imperative that you understand that God and His truth are beyond everything in this world. That is why nothing in this world is real, and why it is meaningless in and of itself.

Because there is no hierarchy of illusions—the Holy Spirit's answer to the ego's first law of chaos that the truth must be different for everyone (T-23.II.2)—nothing in the world is better or worse than anything else, nothing is holier or unholier than anything else. Nothing is nothing. Whether you think something—tangible or intangible—is of great, little, or no magnitude, it is still nothing. If you cannot accept this principle at least at the conceptual level, you will, again, get trapped in the ego thought system by making the error of separation real. This means making the body real, and having worldly life, not to mention your participation in it, become significant. In making the separation real, you inevitably get caught up in the kinds of things that troubled Hamlet: the inevitability of death, one's own guilt and fear, yearning to escape from the world, and, finally, imagining what goes on after we die—"*what dreams may come*" (III,i,66).

(2:1) In this perception of the universe as God created it, it would be impossible to think of Him as loving.

This is the same idea as that expressed at the beginning of Chapter 13, where Jesus says that the world is "the delusional system of those made mad by guilt" (T-13.in.2:2). After describing what this world is really like in terms of its pain and suffering, he concludes: "If this were the real world, God *would* be cruel" (T-13.in.3:1).

(2:2) For who has decreed that all things pass away, ending in dust and disappointment and despair, can but be feared.

Jesus is describing the theology of the ego thought system. The result of believing in separation, sin, guilt, and fear is the belief that God has decreed that everything here will end in "dust and disappointment and despair." (Note, incidentally, Jesus' use of the alliterative *d*.) This is the message of the Adam and Eve story in Genesis—because we have sinned, we will forevermore remain in fear of a punishing God. And we must believe this God will punish us because we believe in the reality of the world and our own existence—a self of sin and guilt, deserving punishment.

Returning to Hamlet's soliloquy, *"To be, or not to be"* in the sense of "to exist, or not to exist" is *not* the question, because there *is* no existence. How could we choose existence or non-existence when there is no existence to begin with? When we understand *A Course in Miracles'* definition of *being* and its use of the word *be*, we can see that the right-minded way of looking at this is: *"To be, or not to be"* *is* the question. *To be*, as the Course talks about it, means "the state of being, which is Heaven." Working with that definition, this is the only question that makes sense: "Do I choose to deny the Being of Christ as my Identity, which the Atonement principle holds out to me, or do I deny the denial of that Being, having first chosen the existence of the ego?" With the Course's definition, *not to be* means "to exist as an individual—an ego." Recall Jesus' distinction between being and existence cited earlier (T-4.III.3; T-4.VII.4:1-4). While he does not hold consistently to this distinction all the way through the Course, he does at the beginning of the text: *being* is of spirit, and *existence* is of the ego.

Thus, if we understand Hamlet's *"To be, or not to be"* to mean "To exist, or to be: that is the question," from the point of view of *A Course in Miracles*, it makes perfect sense. That, again, is the only real question.

If I choose the ego, I am choosing existence, which is not being. Or if I choose the Holy Spirit, I am choosing to remember Being, my reality as Christ. And so the good news is that we are one with God in Being, or Heaven; and because God is not in the realm of existence, neither are we. We are an idea in the Mind of God, which has never left its Source in His Mind.

Jesus now continues with the ego's theology:

(2:3-4) He holds your little life in his hand but by a thread, ready to break it off without regret or care, perhaps today. Or if he waits, yet is the ending certain.

We know that human life is quite precarious. A person may seem to be perfectly healthy, yet all of a sudden drop dead of a heart attack, or have a massive stroke. One could be a passenger on an airplane that crashes, or be killed by a runaway car while crossing the street, or be hit at an intersection while stopped for a light. We are subject to all kinds of what are sometimes referred to as "acts of God": e.g., hurricanes and earthquakes, or a meteor hitting the planet. The body is fragile and vulnerable because it was made that way to reinforce the idea that we deserve to suffer, be punished, and die. Again, Jesus is saying to us: "To think that a loving God would be involved with this is insane." This is why he tells us throughout *A Course in Miracles* how insane we are.

(2:5) Who loves such a god knows not of love, because he has denied that life is real.

The god of the ego is not a god of love, and therefore our fear is justified. At the beginning, in that instant when we believed we killed God to establish ourselves as creators of life, we believed we sinned. Our belief and the guilt that went with it demanded we make up a god of punishment; a god to be feared. That ego god became our substitute for the true Creator.

(2:6) Death has become life's symbol.

This is a reference to what the ego tells us is life, not a reference to real life. Life as a body is a shadow, projected by the ego thought system in the mind. It has meaning only because of death. Remember, the ruling principle of ego life is the reality of opposites. There was God, and there was my separated self, which destroyed Him because we could not both live. Oneness and separation are opposites and cannot coexist. If I am to exist as a separate individual, God had to be killed. My life then derived its meaning from the death of God because my life had been purchased through His death. In a statement that has become quite well known, St. Paul said that "the wages of sin is death" (Romans 6:23). The sin of separating from God meant not only that God had to be killed, but that I would have to be killed as punishment for my sin.

(2:6-8) Death has become life's symbol. His world is now a battleground, where contradiction reigns and opposites make endless war. Where there is death is peace impossible.

Because death has become life's symbol, the world has become a battleground. In my mind "life" is now a struggle against Life. Only one will survive. I believe I killed God, but there He is in my mind. If I am alive, *along with God*, it is only an instant before I am destroyed by Him. That is the ego's fear, which is why it counsels us to make up a world in which we can be concealed and protected. There will come a moment when we realize that the god of vengeance, the threat of death, the gun pointed at our head, is not coming from outside. The pointed gun is held by us! We are responsible for fear. Referring to that instant, a line in the workbook says: "This moment can be terrible" (W-pI.170.8:1). The gun is our own guilt, which tells us our fate is inevitable; we will be annihilated. Thus the confrontation of life with Life very quickly becomes a struggle between life and death. One of us will die and the other will live. It is always *one or the other*. Since the struggle—the battleground—is in our minds, that is what is projected and becomes the world. In the next paragraph we will see that graphically portrayed, but to repeat: "His world is now a battleground, where contradiction reigns and opposites make endless war. Where there is death is peace impossible."

To continue our discussion, in this world opposites reign: good and evil, life and death. In truth—in oneness—it is not possible to have *both* good and evil. Good is only good. There can be no evil there. Good is part of love and is totally one. Likewise in truth, life is life; there is no death there. But in this world there is life in death. One is going to die and the other will live. In the end I am going to die because God is going to live, according to the ego. And so there is endless war, which *is* the nature of the world. Where this endless war between life and death exists, peace is impossible, which is why there has never been peace in this world and there never will be, until the cause of war is undone at its source: the guilt-ridden mind.

War started the instant there was consciousness, awareness of differences, life and death, and organisms that had to feed off one another in order to survive. Ego life is predatory. The law of nature is kill or be killed, devour or be devoured. In order to exist, a living organism must feed off some other organism. I discussed this fundamentally important point earlier, and we are going to see it graphically described in the next paragraph. Feeding off God and draining His life's blood so we could have it is how our existence began. This then became the "law of nature" in our minds. That is why the world is what it is. That is why we made bodies that are not self-sufficient and can exist *only* by feeding off what is outside: oxygen, water, nutrition. The sense of lack that demands we become predators is not only true of our physical bodies, but of our psychological bodies as well. We need love, attention, and caring from other people. We need them to be sensitive to, and thoughtful of our needs. Thus we feed off others psychologically—the special relationship—which is no different from our feeding off other forms of "life" on the physical level.

From all that we have been saying, therefore, it is abundantly clear that the ego thought system in our minds is filled with horror. But it would be a mistake to feel guilty as we continue to look at what is in our minds. That would merely perpetuate the problem. Obviously we are here because we have accepted the ego thought system, but once we have identified the problem, which Hamlet failed to do, we are in a position to correct it. Our guilt protects the problem from its resolution. Hence, Jesus says to us in the text:

> ...trust implicitly your willingness, whatever else may enter. Concentrate only on this, and be not disturbed that shadows surround it. That is why you came. If you could come without them you would not need the holy instant (T-18.IV.2:3-6).

Jesus asks us not to be upset because of the shadows cast by our guilt: shadows of hate and fear. That is why we came. We brought the shadows with us. At some point, after we have looked carefully enough to see the nature and origin of these shadows, we might then be able to say and truly mean: "There must be another way." That is the invitation to have Jesus help us look at the shadows to recognize that their source is not in the body or the world. Their source lies in our minds' decision *to believe* in the shadows of hatred, death, and specialness. And because we made the decision, we now can change it. It is therefore helpful to step back and see the world for what it is, because that is the beginning of undoing its source in our minds; that is the beginning of forgiveness.

This next paragraph clarifies even further the nature of these shadows. As announcers sometimes say when they introduce a movie or a new broadcast: "The following material contains some graphic images that may not be suitable for children." The reader is forewarned:

(3:1) Death is the symbol of the fear of God.

I have discussed this extensively already. Death symbolizes the fear of God because God is going to kill me for killing Him. My identity, existence, and life were taken from God, and so He had to die so I could have life as a separate individual. I now in turn will pay the price of life by also dying. I am afraid of God, therefore, because I know I shall lose my life to Him. Indeed, everyone around me has; everyone throughout history has. Jesus even tells us in *A Course in Miracles* that sickness is a little form of death (T-27.I.4:8), and everyone gets sick. On seeing the skull of Yorick, his father's jester and dear playmate of the young prince—"*Alas, poor Yorick!–I knew him*"—Hamlet muses in his typical melancholic fashion on the transient futility of life:

> *Here hung those lips that I have kist I know not how oft. Where be*
> *your gibes now? your gambols? your songs? your flashes of*
> *merriment, that were wont to set the table on a roar? Not one now,*
> *to mock your own grinning? quite chop-faln?* (V,i,189)

Chop-faln is an archaic word meaning "dejected" or "dispirited."

We thus are haunted by this fear of God. As Jesus says earlier in the manual: "Think not He has forgotten" (M-17.7:4). The ego says: "Don't think for one moment that God has forgotten what you did to Him." Everything in this world reminds us of our sin, and beneath our experience is the terrifying thought that says: "Think not He has forgotten."

This world was made to reassure us that God *did* forget. We may see the wrath of God all around us, but in our desperation we believe that God's wrath is directed against all the bad people, the evildoers, the guilty sinners—anyone and everyone but ourselves. That is why, in part, religions were formed: so we can be good and holy, while others—those who have not "accepted the faith"—are bad, the ones God will punish.

(3:2) His love is blotted out in the idea, which holds it from awareness like a shield held up to obscure the sun.

Death is a defense. It is important to read the lines in *A Course in Miracles* very carefully, because Jesus is often telling us something unusual to our ordinary way of thinking, or that contains subtle implications we might easily miss. Here he tells us the *purpose* of death is to defend against the Love of God; it is a shield whose purpose is to block out the light of love, always present in our right minds. God's Love is like sunlight reflected within. The ego fears that light, and seeks to block it out so that we could never choose to turn towards it. First the light is covered over with the shield of death: the shadows of guilt, hate, and fear, all of which arise from the idea of death. These dark thoughts are then projected to make up another shield: the world and the body. Thus are we doubly shielded from the light.

(3:3) The grimness of the symbol is enough to show it cannot coexist with God.

It cannot coexist with God, that is, unless you believe in an insane god, as, unfortunately, most people do. The early Gnostics got it right, teaching that the biblical God is what they referred to as a "false God." They knew that the true God could not be the biblical figure, for He was beyond the world's insanity. There is a wonderful Gnostic passage that describes God in biblical terms such as wrathful, jealous, vengeful, etc.[7] The passage, in effect, concludes with the question: "What kind of God is this Who gets angry and jealous, demanding sacrifice and death?" Jesus' meaning here is the same: "This fearful God of death cannot be the Creator. Look at the grimness of death. Look at what it symbolizes: pain, suffering, guilt, punishment, and vengeance. How could this have anything to do with a loving God?"

Jesus is therefore asking us to do what he refers to at the beginning of Chapter 24: to look at and question every value that we hold (T-24.in.2:1-2). We are asked to examine what it is we believe about ourselves, the world, and God. He is saying that if we look carefully at our accustomed beliefs we will realize we have believed in an insane God. We believe He is insane because we believe we exist and that the

---

7. See my *Love Does Not Condemn: The World, the Flesh, and the Devil According to Platonism, Christianity, Gnosticism, and A COURSE IN MIRACLES*, pp. 139f.

world is real, as does He. And we must believe we are our bodies or we would not have shown up here.

Now Jesus gets more graphic in discussing the grim symbolism of death:

(3:4) It holds an image of the Son of God in which he is "laid to rest" in devastation's arms, where worms wait to greet him and to last a little while by his destruction.

If you think this is awful, wait until we come to the passage in *Hamlet*, from which this is taken! I warn you, again, this is even more graphic.

This sentence tells us is that if we look carefully at life, we cannot miss seeing that life ends in death, where our dead bodies become food for worms. Just as we maintain our life in the body by feeding off other life forms, when we die we become food for worms and other predatory life. We will be "laid to rest" in devastation's arms, where worms wait to greet us. The worms "last a little while by our destruction," until they in turn are destroyed so that other organisms can eat. Life's tale is always *one or the other*: I live by eating something else. When I die, something else eats me and will live on for a little while until it, too, gets eaten.

(3:5-6) Yet the worms as well are doomed to be destroyed as certainly. And so do all things live because of death.

In these sentences Jesus is not talking about the body alone. He is using the body as a symbol. He is talking about the ego's *thought* of life, which is death. The life of the ego—the birth of individual existence—arose from death, or fed off what had been life, which then, in the warped thinking of the ego, became death. In reality, of course, this individual existence, this parody of life, never happened. But in our wrong-minded dream we believed we destroyed our Source and obtained life at His expense. In our wrong-minded fantasies—which became our reality—we stole His life, took His love, and robbed Him of His power to create. We then believed this power was ours, thus becoming self-created and using our stolen power to "create"; i.e., *mis*-create special love.

God created Heaven by extending Himself as Thought. We "created" the cosmos by projecting the thought system of the ego. That fooled even Plato, who described the world of time as a moving image of eternity. He should have said that it is a moving image of *death*. But our ego wants us to think of the cosmos as eternal, with everything here being marvelous, mysteriously cosmic, and so miraculously grand that only God could have created it. The truth is that only the ego could have done it. The ego god is the miscreator of death, and the illusion of a life that feeds on death. Needless to say, the ego god is really ourselves; its world is our dream, and we are the dreamer. Just as we dream fantastic things at night, the cosmos is a collective and fantastic dream in our shared and delusional minds.

(3:6-8) And so do all things live because of death. Devouring is nature's "law of life." God is insane, and fear alone is real.

What is most important about a passage like this is that it so starkly indicates the nature of the world. If you open your eyes it will be obvious. To repeat, you cannot have physical life without feeding off something else, and you cannot survive as an individual without seizing psychological nurturing from another. The point of looking at these facts is not to have you feel guilty. The fact of our physical and psychological dependency, with its concomitant exploitation, is not something to invest with guilt, for that would establish a reality that is not there. Our predatory ego nature is not sinful; just a case of mistaken identity. It is something to look at, because it will give you pause. You might look at it, for example, and conclude: "You know, this world is not such a nice place." This questioning of our perceptions, the first step in forgiveness, allows us to continue the process until our minds are fully healed.

Devouring is the law of nature and intrinsic to life in the body. The situation would indeed be hopeless if the body and death were real. It is not hopeless because this world of death is a thought in our minds, a defense against something else that is there: love. In our power to change our minds lies our real hope. It is important not to get caught in the illusion that there is hope in the world by thinking that life here would work if only things would change: if only we elected the right president or prime minister; if only our governments had the right policies; if only everyone studied *A Course in Miracles*; if only, if only, if only… This is insane. It is only if you personally elect and choose a different thought system in your mind that there is hope. Meaningful change can take place there; peace will inevitably follow.

Remember, the only meaningful choice is between the thought systems of life and death. It is not a choice between life and death of the body, as Hamlet thought. It is a choice between accepting the true life of God, or believing in the ego, which is tantamount to believing in the death of God. The only meaningful change is a change of mind, the essence of the miracle. Change in the world is meaningless because that is just changing illusions, what Freud referred to as symptom substitution. Without the switch from the ego to the Holy Spirit, we are condemned to eat and be eaten, and then what devours us will in turn be devoured, and on and on and on it goes.

Before turning to this remarkable passage from *Hamlet*, the basis for the passage we have just examined on death's cycle of devouring and being devoured, I might mention that there is other evidence of *Hamlet's* influence on *A Course in Miracles* as well. The most notable of these is the important section "The Two Pictures" in Chapter 17 of the text. There Jesus talks about the picture of light offered by the Holy Spirit, in contrast to the ego's picture of death. Both pictures are placed in frames, which Jesus also contrasts. The ego's picture of death is set in the glitter-filled frame—the special relationship—that is wonderful to look at, so attractive in fact that no one really looks at the picture itself. On the other hand, the Holy Spirit's picture—the holy relationship or the holy instant—is so lightly framed that we go right to the picture itself, there to see the radiant light of God. Jesus emphatically appeals to us: "Look at the *picture*. Do not let the frame distract you" (T-17.IV.9:1-2).

The metaphor of the two pictures is taken from the scene between Hamlet and Gertrude, where the prince confronts his mother with the truth of hid father's murder, which she evidently did not know about. Hamlet shows her two pictures: *"Hyperion to a satyr"* (I,ii,140), Hyperion here used synonymously with Apollo. It is that comparison with the two pictures that happily found its way into the Course.

Now to the promised passage from *Hamlet*. It appears in Act Four, scene three, which follows Hamlet's killing of Polonius, the father of Ophelia, whom Hamlet loves but ends up mistreating. Polonius is a lord in the court, but often comes across as an old fool, and Hamlet has no use for him. Polonius was spying on Hamlet as he entered Gertrude's chamber to confront his mother. He hides, but Hamlet, hearing rustling behind the curtain, impulsively thrusts his sword through the concealed figure, suspecting it is Claudius. But alas, the king lives and the innocent Polonius falls. In the next scene Claudius asks his stepson/nephew:

Now, Hamlet, where's Polonius?

Hamlet replies:

At supper.

Claudius:

At supper! where?

Hamlet:

Not where he eats, but where he is eaten: a certain convocation of politic worms are e'en at him.

Hamlet's meaning is that even now as we are speaking, the worms are at work.
  He continues:

Your worm is your only emperor for diet: we fat all creatures else to fat us,

We eat creatures; otherwise they will eat us.
  And so:

and we fat ourselves for maggots:

We eat and fatten ourselves. Then we die, and the maggots fatten themselves by eating us.
  Thus are king and beggar equalized:

your fat king and your lean beggar is but variable service,–two dishes, but to one table: that's the end.

Whether rich or poor, fat or thin, you are going to end up being eaten.
  The king then exclaims, knowing that Hamlet is on to him, and suspects some trick:

Alas, alas!

But there is no stopping our prince:

A man may fish with the worm that hath eat of a king,

So the king dies, and is eaten by the worm.
  Now the man uses the worm as bait to catch fish, itself to be eaten; and on and on the cycle goes:

and eat of the fish that hath fed of that worm.

The king asks:

What dost thou mean by this?

And Hamlet says scornfully:

Nothing but to show you how a king may go a progress through the guts of a beggar.

(IV,iii,17)

We are all the same; constantly feeding off each other: eating as we are eaten, eaten as we eat.

Hamlet's cynical and sardonic observations are the basis for the passage in the manual, as I have said. We can see why Hamlet is not only a tragic figure, but a figure with almost universal appeal. He speaks openly about what everyone knows but is loathe to admit. As Jesus says in Lesson 182, referring to being an alien in this world: "No one but knows whereof we speak" (W-pI.182.2:1). On some level we all know we are not at home here, and do not belong; on some level we all know the truth about the body. Hamlet was obsessed with this truth, and was horrified by the world and repulsed by the body. From the point of view of *A Course in Miracles*, the tragic part of his character is that he does not know a way out. Hamlet, again, is everyman. Most of us do not know a way out, either.

When we read something like this—whether in Shakespeare, the manual for teachers, or other places in *A Course in Miracles*—and then think about it, it is astounding to realize how so very few openly acknowledge the ugliness, desperation, and futility of life. We do not allow ourselves to look honestly upon the world or ourselves. Instead, we pretty things over. That is what Freud was pointing to when he told his daughter, to repeat his wise words: "Things are not so lovely behind those lovely facades." We all try to disguise the ugliness of the world and body behind the lovely facades of our special relationships.

Let us remember, however, that the world and body are not ugly in and of themselves, for of themselves they are nothing but meaningless shadows. What establishes their ugliness is the thought of murder that gave rise to them in the first place; the thought we continue to harbor in our minds. We will see again and again that the way out of Hamlet's dilemma—which is the way out for all of us—is to realize that death is a thought we have chosen in our minds. But we cannot have that realization until we first *look* at the projections of that thought. This looking is the heart of forgiveness, as the workbook reminds us: "Forgiveness … is still, and quietly does nothing…. It merely looks, and waits, and judges not" (W-pII.1.4:1,3).

To counter the Holy Spirit's forgiveness the ego attempts to convince us the sins we perceive in others are real; namely, our projections are true. Shortly before the lines I just quoted from the workbook, Jesus describes the ego's strategy: "The [unforgiving] thought protects projection…" (W-pII.1.2:3). These unforgiving thoughts include all thoughts of specialness—love and hate. These are the judgments of others we never raise to the forgiving light of truth, for they are protected by our certainty they are justified and therefore true. Thus we have made the world seem even more real by these unforgiving thoughts. As long as we take our special relationships seriously by making judgments about them, we will never know the world seems real *only* because we have wanted it to be real. Thus is our ego's purpose fulfilled by protecting the underlying thoughts of guilt and death in our minds.

To restate this: We made up the world as a defense in order to escape our original unforgiving and guilt-ridden thought against God. The world shields us from recognizing that ontological thought of murder by separating from our Victim. If we do not see the guilt, the ego tells us, it is not there. Thus we take the world very seriously, and strive to make its seeming reality even more real. We do not want to recognize the fact that the world is but a projection of the mind, the source of the real problem.

In the all-important section of the text titled "The Substitute Reality," we find perhaps the best account of the original projection and fragmentation that made the world. In that section Jesus says that "[the world] was the first projection of error outward" (T-18.I.6:1). By "error" he means the original separation thought that substituted our life for God's. He then continues by saying: "The world arose to hide it [the projection]…." (T-18.I.6:2). The projection of error displaced onto others the inner thoughts of separation, guilt, and death, allowing us to say: "It is not my thoughts. They are outside me—in others." The world and the body—filled with our unforgiving thoughts—arose as screens behind which is hidden the dynamic of projection. Unseen, it remains uncorrected; uncorrected, it protects the mind's thoughts of guilt and death. Therefore, if we are not aware of the fact that the world is a projection, we will never be able to change the thought that gave rise to it. The original unforgiving thought in our minds remains, covered over by the world and the unforgiving judgments we make through our special relationships.

The value of honestly looking at the horrifying nature of the world is in finally being able to say: "There is no hope here; there must be another way." How can there be hope in a world that is literally an expression of guilt—made by and from guilt? This hopeless world is replete with expressions of "kill or be killed": devouring, stealing, and cannibalizing as each of us lives to satisfy our insatiable appetite for specialness, the core of our individual identity. Being able to see through the projection and honestly say "There must be another way!" is what will motivate us sincerely to call upon the Teacher Who represents the "other way" in our minds. The Holy Spirit will show us that what we are seeing and judging outside in the world—the "law of nature": killing and devouring—is coming from the thoughts of sin and guilt in our minds that are themselves a defense against the Love of God.

The resplendent light of God's Love is blotted out by the idea of death, which holds It from our awareness like a shield held up to obscure the sun. The outer world of murder, hate, pain, and death is a *defense* against the inner world of murder, hate, pain, and death. In turn, the inner world is a *defense* against the principle of the Atonement that is in our minds, blocked from our awareness by these two shields, the double shield of oblivion referred to in the workbook (W-pI.136.5:2). Looking honestly at the ego's system of defenses is our only hope. Without it we are condemned to go through the endless cycles of sin, guilt, fear, and death—both in the mind and in the projected world.

As we have seen, the first paragraph of "What Is Death?" describes the true nature of the world: "The cyclical, the changing and unsure; the undependable and the unsteady, waxing and waning...." (M-27.1:6). This world is sustained by the law of devouring: worms eating dead flesh; other creatures eating the worms; and everyone devouring everyone and everything else.

Let us return to Hamlet and the graveyard scene, where he was last seen bemoaning the fate of his beloved Yorick. He continues his fascination with the rotting corpses, and asks Horatio about the fate of the noble Alexander and imperious Caesar, whose greatness has been reduced to the dust that would eventually find its way to plugging wine casks, beer barrels, or protective walls:

To what base uses we may return, Horatio! Why may
not imagination trace the noble dust of Alexander
till he find it stopping a bung-hole?

Horatio tries to demur, but Hamlet persists:

No, faith, not a jot; but to follow him thither with
modesty enough, and likelihood to lead it: as
thus; Alexander died, Alexander was buried,
Alexander returneth into dust; the dust is earth: of
earth we make loam; and why of that loam whereto he
was converted might they not stop a beer-barrel?
Imperious Caesar, dead and turn'd to clay,
Might stop a hole to keep the wind away:
O, that that earth, which kept the world in awe
Should patch a wall to expel the winter's flaw!

(V,i,209)

So much for life in the body, however filled with greatness or grandeur it may have been.

We cannot get to the light until we go through the darkness of separation, death, and guilt, because, again, we made the darkness real and then an outer world to shield us from that inner darkness. We then say: "But it is not a darkened world. It is a lovely, beautiful world. It may have some bad things in it, to be sure, but it is an amazing, wondrous place nonetheless. There may be a few bad people here, to be sure, but we shall soon rid the world of them so that we can live together in peace and harmony."

It does not matter on which side you are on political or social issues—everyone does the same thing. We strive to maintain the illusion that we are beings of light and love—spokespersons for the truth. *A Course in Miracles* is telling us that no one here is a spokesperson for the truth, because truth is not of this world. Any reflection of truth—if it is genuine—must embrace *all* people in its vision. True life is *one*. It is not divisible. The Life of God cannot be separated into many. Any reflection of truth in the dream must be in a form that embraces all people, without exception, seeing all parts of the Sonship as sharing a common interest. If any part is excluded in our thought, we immediately know the ego is its source. To return to the graphic imagery of *Hamlet* and the manual, such exclusionary judgment is simply another version of the law of devouring: worms eating bodies, then being eaten

54

by other bodies. The good will establish their goodness by condemning those perceived as evil. Thus they get fat through feasting on their brothers' innocence, only to be attacked in return.

In the world of guilt and death, victimizers vanquish victims and then become victims in turn. Those who were once victims achieve power by taking it from their victimizers. They then devour them and grow fat until they themselves are vanquished. History abounds with examples, such as the French Revolution, while it is a virtual truism in mental health circles that abused children grow up to become abusing adults. The cycle is unending. Once again, nothing in this world—nothing we think is alive in this world—can exist without feeding off something else. It must be that way, because the world began with the thought: "I can exist only by feeding off God."

The good news is that all this is an illusion; nothing but a dream. The bad news is that we believe it; but then pretend we do not. We do not look honestly and objectively at the horror of this system of devouring. We disguise its ugliness. We take life in the world seriously, and then try to make it meaningful, beautiful, holy, and good. Passages such as the ones we have been reviewing—of which there are many throughout *A Course in Miracles*—show us the underside, the ugly thought of murder and guilt that is behind the "lovely facade." If you do not reach that thought, there is truly no hope.

A Course in Miracles is valuable to us because it offers the only legitimate hope that exists in the world: namely, the message that the world we see is a mirror reflecting what is inside, "the witness to your state of mind, the outside picture of an inward condition" (T-21.in.1:5). Our perceptions reflect what we are afraid to look at in our minds, and therefore do not want to see. Jesus says to us: "If you let me help you perceive the world through my eyes, however, I will show you the guilt your world is covering, and the love covered by the guilt. When you truly look with me, and take my hand as we go through the clouds of guilt to the light beyond, everything will change."

Honestly looking at the ugliness and the cannibalism we call life can be nauseating. It is only natural that we would be upset by reading graphic descriptions of what lies behind the facade, since we identify with our bodies. The idea of being consumed by worms after we are dead is not very pleasant to consider. The cycle of devouring—the ego's "law of nature"—is upsetting because we have bought into the ego strategy that requires the belief we are bodies. Once that identification is secure, we exist in a perpetual state of mindlessness—with no awareness of what has happened. We assume we are bodies governed by brains, subject to influences that are beyond our control—our genetic makeup, for example. We are not aware we are mindless because we do not have a concept of mind. Almost all scientists assume that mind is somehow an activity of the brain. That is not what *A Course in Miracles* means by *mind*, which is not in the body, nor is it located anywhere in time and space. Mind projects thoughts, and the body is but one of those projections. Thus does mind gives rise to the illusion of a body, and governs it behind the scenes.

Since it is virtually impossible for us *not* to identify with the body—after all we are even reading these words with eyes, and understanding them with a brain—it is virtually impossible to identify with the mind. As we so easily assume we are bodies, when we carefully study passages from "What Is Death?" in the manual, along with parallel passages from *Hamlet*, we are bound to be upset. That is why death, the theme of this book, is so upsetting. We believe that death marks the end of our existence, and we would do anything and everything to defend against the anxiety this inevitably arouses in us.

Fortunately, there is a right-minded view of this situation, even of the nausea that one might experience from our discussion. Our disgust at the ego's viciousness calls attention to the fact that we have identified with the body. Further, by looking closely at what the body is and what it does, and then looking at the revulsion we feel, we recognize that we are being given a clue—if we ask the right teacher—about the body's true origins in the mind. In other words, when we ask Jesus for help, when we finally throw up our hands in dismay, despair, and disgust, saying, "There must be another way, another teacher who can help me with my experience," his answer, on the level of content—which has nothing to do with the way we experience the answer—is to have us realize the world we perceive as real *outside* is a picture of a world we have made real *inside*. The overriding thrust of the early lessons in the workbook is to have us understand that the reason the objects in the room, for example, mean nothing, is that we have projected our own thinking onto them. Those lessons thus have as their specific goal our learning there is both an inner and an outer world, the latter being the projection of the former.

We can see, therefore, that right at the beginning of the 365-day mind-training program constituting the workbook we are asked to think in specific terms about *A Course in Miracles'* fundamental message: the mind makes the body, and what we perceive outside is nothing more or less than a projection of what we have made real inside. Again, *ideas leave not their source*; this principle cannot be stated often enough. While it is not specifically articulated in the early lessons, it does come up later on, as we will see, and it is of course discussed extensively in the text. This principle is so crucial to our learning the Course that we are asked early in the workbook to consider the idea that it is our thoughts that make up the world, which is why Jesus later states: "There is no world!" (W-pI.132.6:2).

The importance of *ideas leave not their source* for our discussion is that it helps us understand that death is of the mind, not the body. Death is a thought. Our anxiety about the body, its fate, and the devouring nature of life can serve a useful purpose in that it would force us to ask for help. This comes in the form of being shown over and over again, day in and day out, that what we perceive outside is coming from a decision in our minds. As we think about that fact more and more, as we increasingly see its validity, we can begin detaching from our egos. Thus are we better able to step back from our wrong minds and watch what we do.

In this regard, I hope you can objectively look at the world. That is why we have been reading these passages. Step back and look at the nature of the world and body, and what it means to be living here. The more you can look without the ego, the more objective you can be about the body; and the more you can recognize the sheer insanity of physical life. One more time: murder and death cannot possibly have anything to do with God.

Stated another way, the part of you that steps back and looks without judgment at the body's functioning—and how specifically *you* function as a body—is *not* the body. Thus right-minded perception begins the process of breaking your identification with the body and with the ego thought system. If you are looking without guilt and fear, and without any judgments whatsoever—simply saying: "Yes, that is the nature of the body"—you cannot be looking with your ego, because judgment is the ego's middle name. You are truly looking when the decision maker in your mind joins with Jesus, seeing through his eyes of forgiveness. Such vision constitutes being in one's right mind; the essence of asking the Holy Spirit for help. You simply look at what goes on here and real-ize its terrible nature. That will spur the process of re-directing your attention from the world to the decision-making part of your mind, wherein lies your only hope.

"There is one life and that I share with God"—I

We are now going to consider some workbook passages that specif-ically address the idea that death is a thought in the mind. In his *"To be, or not to be"* speech, Hamlet fell into the ego's trap of believing that death is of the body and is therefore real, a trap to which we all are prey. As I have been saying, *"To be, or not to be"* is not a question. It is the ego's statement that affirms the body's reality, and the body's serious problem, which is death. The real problem, however, has nothing to do with the body at all. *The real problem is guilt.* The body and death are projections of the guilt that is in the mind, and as long as we focus on the body we can never return to the problem's true source. Thus we are condemned to think that death is real, part of the natural state of things in the world. It is, of course, except that since the world is an illusion, death is a natural state of nothing.

We begin with Lesson 167, "There is one life and that I share with God," paragraph 3.

(W-pI.167.3:1-2) You think that death is of the body. Yet it is but an idea, irrelevant to what is seen as physical.

This means nothing to us as long as we think our bodies are real. And Jesus is more than aware of the fact that all of us find it very diffi-cult to relate to statements like this. We may relate to these words intel-lectually, but it is quite another thing to think of ourselves as unreal, to accept that the self we see every morning in the mirror, that we dress, feed, rest, and recreate is simply a projection of a thought, and an illu-sory thought at that.

When you are asleep at night having a dream, your experiences seem very real. The people and their actions seem so real in fact that you may have the same reactions as when you are awake: happy, sad, excited, terrified, depressed. Within the dream it all seems so true. It is only when you awaken that you realize it was a dream. Likewise, our experience in the world is a dream; and it is very difficult to understand that nothing is happening here at all, being nothing but the mind's projection.

As you go through your day—without trying to impose anything on yourself; without trying to spiritualize the meaning of events; without trying to deny your body's feelings or emotions—try to remember the ego's strategy of having you focus on your body instead of your mind. When you are confronted with death, whether it is the death of someone you know, the death of people in another part of the world, or your own, be aware as you go through the "normal" experience of fear and grief that this is not happening to the body at all. Remember: "You think that death is of the body. Yet it is but an idea, irrelevant to what is seen as physical." Death is nothing but thought in your mind. As best you can, try to step back with Jesus and watch yourself be like everyone else, having all the feelings that are natural and normal in the world when dealing with sickness and death. Do not deny what you are thinking and feeling, but try to remember that there *is* another way of thinking.

I was asked for advice by someone attending this workshop about how to deal with his sister's recent diagnosis of cancer, and his own ambivalence about life and death. He knew he was witnessing his own dream as well as his sister's, but he found it confusing to try to understand how to deal with this situation in terms of her responsibility and his own for the events in the dream. In my response I stressed that the most important aspect of studying *A Course in Miracles*—indeed its nuts and bolts—comes in applying it to the circumstances of our everyday lives. The first rule to follow is not to deny what you are thinking or feeling. This can be summed up very simply by saying that the first "law" for a student of *A Course in Miracles* is to be normal. Normal people become upset when a loved one has cancer, or any other life-threatening disease. That type of situation brings up issues, thoughts, and feelings in all of us. The last thing in the world that would be helpful is to push them away, or attempt to put a spiritual cover over them by saying: "This is her choice, as well as my own. Besides, it is all a dream and is not even happening"; and so on. On the metaphysical level it is true that we choose our life scripts, but we would not be here in this body if we did not believe the exact opposite: *the world chose us.* Therefore we must allow the ego to do its thing before it can be corrected and undone.

I went on to explain:

Once you have honored your reactions to these very difficult circumstances, asking for help to look at things differently would be meaningful. Indeed, it is possible, as you go through the anger, hurt, anxiety, guilt, fear, and whatever else comes up for you, to step back and watch yourself react, or at least make the attempt to do so. It is very important to have the little willingness to ask Jesus to help you look at these reactions.

When you attend a workshop, or undertake any serious study of *A Course in Miracles*, one of the reasons things frequently get worse before they get better is that you have to look at your ego: *the problem.* You have to experience your ego before you can move beyond it. And so, when confronted with a circumstance like your sister's cancer, where death is an imminent possibility, you will most likely have all the expected feelings. It is important to be aware of them. As Jesus cautions us early in the text: Denying one's experience in the world is practically impossible, and is "a particularly unworthy form of denial" (T-2.IV.3:8,10-11). Understanding the dynamics of the ego as they are explained throughout the Course can be very helpful, because then you understand what is going on in you, your sister, and your family—realizing that you are part of the same insane thought system shared by all. The more you cultivate an attitude of watching yourself have a reaction—without judgment—the more you obtain a certain detachment from the body, and the thought system of separation that gave rise to it.

In a sense, then, you can have your cake and eat it, too. You respect your feelings without denying them; but you also look at them with an awareness that there is more to this than your feelings. There is an alternative to suffering. As I pointed out earlier, Hamlet did not allow himself that luxury, so he just saw what was awful without seeing an answer. In fact, that is the case with most people. So I suggest that you go through this experience as best you can, as a normal person would, and as much as possible ask for help in looking at what you are feeling, with at least the understanding that those feelings are a defense against truly knowing, as the great Spanish playwright Calderón said: life is a dream.

(3:3-4) A thought is in the mind. It can be then applied as mind directs it.

This is not the first time in the workbook that Jesus makes this kind of statement. Indeed, it is a concept that appears many times throughout *A Course in Miracles*. Even if you find this idea difficult to relate to, it is important at least to try to think about its meaning. *Everything is thought.* "A thought is in the mind. It can be then applied as the mind directs it." This means it can be projected as the mind's decision maker directs—with the ego or the Holy Spirit.

Since the body is merely a projected thought, it is literally lifeless and, like a marionette, does, says, and thinks nothing—unless its strings are pulled and a human voice speaks its words. Jesus says in many places in the Course that the body does not feel; it is not born, nor does it die; it does not get sick nor well; its brain does not think, its eyes do not see, its ears do not hear. In fact, the body does absolutely nothing.[8] A puppet does not do anything, either, but it can be made to look as if it were reacting to something it sees or hears, or as if it were happy or sad, growing old, or even dying. The body is no different. Even though this goes directly against our experience, it is helpful at the beginning— and the beginning can last for many years—to understand that all our experiences are being played out somewhere else—not in our bodies but in our minds. Without that understanding there is no hope. Would you place your hope in a lifeless piece of wood? Yet that is what we all do because we are unaware of the mind's existence, the puppeteer behind the scenes that directs everything the puppet does.

The reason we do not want to see this is that we are afraid to be in contact with the mind, where the ego has told us: "God will get you, and you will meet with certain annihilation." In the text we are told: "Loudly the ego tells you not to look inward, for if you do your eyes will light on sin, and God will strike you blind" (T-21.IV.2:3). That is what we all believe, and believed at the beginning. Why? Because the ego told us that our lives were stolen from Life, which left that Life dead. We then possessed the life we stole and killed for, a sin deserving inevitable punishment. Since sin occurred in the mind, so too will the punishment. With no other voice to hear—the Holy Spirit's Voice had been silenced, confined to the ego's vaults of oblivion, guarded by guilt—we believed the ego, adding two and two and ending up with six and seven-eighths. Our next thought was not surprising, given that it was the ego's plan from the beginning: "If we leave the mind, God will never find us; thus we can avoid His vengeful wrath." The ego, of course, never informed us that we *cannot* leave the mind: *Ideas leave not their source.* We are always in our minds; there is nothing else.

---

8. See, for example: T-28.V.4-5; T-28.VI.2; W-pI.92.1-2.

The terror of being punished by God is in our minds, but, being mindless, we are no longer aware of it. Yet does this terror cast its ugly shadow beyond the veil that separates the mind from the body, and we experience the effects of our guilt, fear, and hate, with no knowledge of their source. Because of this lack of awareness, because we are programmed by the ego to see judgment and sin only outside, our eyes see only external problems. We thus can say with full conviction: "Problems are not in me, but in everyone else. Everyone and everything are the cause of my distress."

This is why, when confronted with choices regarding the problems in the world, we, like Hamlet, ask the wrong question. We always ask the wrong question, whether we confront a problem we think is of great magnitude like Hamlet's "*To be, or not to be,*" or problems of lesser magnitude such as: "Should I live in this city?" "Should I remain in this relationship?" "Should I take this job?" "Should I eat this food?" No matter what problems we face in the world, we always ask the wrong questions, which are but statements of a point of view. This, as we discussed before, is that separation, guilt, and death are real, all of which exist outside us. Underlying this statement is the fear that says: "Do not go within!"

As long as we keep asking questions about the world outside, and moreover believe we receive meaningful answers, we will never bother with the world inside. Remember, the only real "*To be, or not to be*" question is: "Do I choose to remember that I am a child of being, or do I continue to believe I am a child of existence?" "Will I be a child of Love or fear; a child of God or the ego?" *That* is the only meaningful question. All the others are pseudo-questions, with no meaningful answers possible. Jesus goes one step further in the section I mentioned earlier, "The Quiet Answer" (T-27.IV), where he says that all questions asked within the world are expressions of hate, because they reinforce our belief in the world, which was made by hate.

We thus continue to protect the thought of hate in our minds that says: "I hate God because He is going to punish me for stealing what is really mine." We defend against that thought by projecting it out to make up a world. All questions here, then, have the purpose of making the world seem real. Therefore, one of the goals of *A Course in Miracles* is for Jesus to help us know the right question to ask. All questions we ask of him about our worldly problems are not questions at all.

Once again, they are statements that defend against the truth and prevent his giving us the only answer that will heal—forgiveness.

Even though it may begin as a mere intellectual exercise, it is very helpful to observe yourself making the body, death, and separation real. The more you practice this self-observation, the more you will see that you make death real any time you try to establish the reality of physical life, since any time you try to preserve life you are essentially saying death is real and life can be threatened. Recall the introduction to the text: *"Nothing real can be threatened. Nothing unreal exists"* (T-in.2:2-3).

As you continue to observe yourself making the error real, the ideas of *A Course in Miracles* will become more and more true for you; not just intellectually, but much more genuinely true as part of your awareness. It is not important that you immediately identify yourself as mind. That takes a lot of work and usually a long time. What is important is that you have the *willingness* to identify as mind; and that you have the little willingness to observe the value you place on the body, meaning the specialness associated with it.

(3:3-5) A thought is in the mind. It can be then applied as mind directs it. But its origin is where it must be changed, if change occurs.

That is a wonderful, wonderful passage! No worms, no streaming blood, no flesh ripped from bone in that sentence. Jesus is telling us that if we want to have meaningful change, it must be in the mind because that is where the thought is. The thought is not in the world, which is nothing but the object of the thought's projection, but in the mind from which it was projected.

To repeat, the idea is to watch yourself trying to change the body. Watch yourself wanting to change the world and everything you get your hands on—or get your thinking around—wanting to change everything *except your mind*. What makes *A Course in Miracles* easy is that Jesus is not asking you to change anyone or anything at all, only yourself. And changing yourself is not difficult when you recognize that all he is asking you to do is change your mind's teacher. When you ask Jesus for help, you need only look with him at your ego. You do not have to change or modify it, let alone let it go or fight against it. Just watch your ego with Jesus. That is the reason he emphasizes that all you need is *a little willingness* (T-18.V.2:5), and why he says his Course is not difficult. What makes it difficult is our resistance to it, born of the fear of setting aside our investment in the body, not to mention our identification with its underlying thought system of specialness. The process of forgiveness is quite straightforward.

Death, therefore, is not something that has to be resolved at the level of the body. You do not have to agonize the way our friend Hamlet did about whether to stay in this world and *"suffer the slings and arrows of outrageous fortune,"* or *"by opposing end them,"* or die, and then have to deal with *"what dreams may come"* (III,i,57).You do not have to evaluate which is going to be worse: suffering in this world only to be punished by God in the end, or dying now and experiencing His immediate punishment. There is nothing to decide, because no bodily state is real. There is no pre-body, present-body, or post-body state. *Everything is in the mind.* The body is nothing, and nothing is in the body. Sometimes people ask where they go when they die. The fact is that you do not go anywhere, because you were never anywhere in the first place. Your mind just dreamily wandered off into a far country called the body, living in the world. But your mind never left its Source. You just dreamt that you did.

Early on in the scribing of *A Course in Miracles*, Jesus said to Helen: "You are much too tolerant of mind wandering...." (T-2.VI.4:6). He was speaking about the wandering of the mind away from itself into the world. But *ideas leave not their source.* This *is* the Course's key concept! The idea of a fearful world has never left its source, which is the thought of fear in the mind; the idea of a death-filled world permeated with devouring and cannibalizing organisms has never left its source, which is the thought of death in the mind. The mind is where the problem is, and that is where it must be solved. At the end of Chapter 5 in the text is found this nugget: "Your part is merely to return your thinking to the point at which the error was made, and give it over to the Atonement in peace" (T-5.VII.6:5).

Miracle is the term Jesus uses for this dynamic of returning problems from the world and body back to the mind. That is why this book is called *A Course in Miracles*. It is not a course in love or truth, but a course in learning to choose the miracle that undoes the blocks to the awareness of love and truth (T-in.1:6-7): "The miracle establishes you dream a dream, and that its content is not true" (T-28.II.7:1). If Hamlet had asked Jesus for help, Jesus would have responded: "You are dreaming of being in a body. The world is so distasteful and fills you with such despair because of the guilt in your mind that you are projecting to make a dream of guilt. But the guilt in your mind is itself part of your dream. What you are dreaming, both of life in a body and life as a guilty thought in your mind, is unreal." Jesus would have continued: "Look with me on the devastation of your mind's thoughts about yourself and your enormous guilt, and let me remind you that what you see is false. Let me help you look within and you will realize these thoughts are only flimsy veils before the light. They have no power to keep its truth away from you." As he says in the workbook: "[The miracle] merely looks on devastation, and reminds the mind that what it sees is false" (W-pII.13.1:3).

The world, and the guilt that made the world, are not solid walls of granite that can block out the light of the sun, which you can spell S-o-n. When you look with Jesus at the shields that seem to block out the light—the outer world of separated forms and the inner world of guilt—the shields disappear. Remember, looking with Jesus means looking without guilt and judgment. When you look at the shields this way, it is apparent they have no power to keep the light of our Identity as Christ from shining in your mind. Your daily practice of *A Course in Miracles* must be aimed at bringing your projections back to their source within. You do this by being aware of your reactions, interpretations, and feelings; of your fears and anxieties; of your specialness, excitement, and anticipation; as well as your concerns about the future. Simply look at all that, realizing they are but projections, and let Jesus help you shift your attention back from the outside picture to the inward condition. That is where the solution lies, and to effect it requires only one simple change: you took a wrong turn toward the ego, and now you are asked to turn back toward to the Holy Spirit. That is all there is to it. That is what is meant by the words we just read: "Its origin is where it must be changed." The thought's origin is in your mind, and only there can meaningful change take place.

In fact, Hamlet himself articulates this shift—the meaning of forgiveness—when he says to his mother in the climactic scene we have already visited:

> *And when you are desirous to be blest,*
> *I'll blessing beg of you.*

(III,iv,172)

65

A pity he did not recognize the import of his words, for they contained the seeds of his own healing. When our guilt becomes so overwhelming that we cry out for a blessing, believing all we deserve is a curse, Jesus' answer is to forgive the one onto whom we have projected our guilt. Looking past the curses we have heaped on the heads of our victim, we see the blessing of Christ that had been veiled by our attack. Seeing it in another reflects our decision to see it in ourselves. And thus we receive the blessing we have offered, and we and our brother are healed as one.

Forgiveness thus returns the blessing *and* curse to their origin in our minds: the curse of death and the blessing of life. Indeed we need come to terms with death, but *in our minds*. It is our *thoughts* about death that have to be changed. The death of the physical body is not important, nor whether there is an afterlife, nor whether we are going to return to the world. How could we return when we were never here in the first place? We did not come into the world nor did we leave it, so how could we come back to it? In *A Course in Miracles* Jesus is talking only of the *mind*, which transcends time and space, which arose when the first projection occurred. The mind's projection of the belief in separation, in sin, guilt, and fear, gave rise to a physical world of past, present, and future. The mind itself is beyond these illusions.

Again, what Jesus is asking us is simply to be aware that the problem is not outside, and we need not agonize, as Hamlet did, over the wrong decision based on the wrong problem. The ego makes up multitudinous and imaginary problems, and each of them, in one way or another, has to do with the body. Needless to say, very high on this list of imaginary problems is death, our great preoccupier. Death, then, becomes *the* problem, forcing us to deal with it. This we do by rationalizing, spiritualizing, denying, becoming fearful, and feeling guilty—all of which will not work. They are distractions from turning our attention inward, the process of forgiveness that *will* work.

Now comes our famous line:

(3:6-7) Ideas leave not their source. The emphasis this course has placed on that idea is due to its centrality in our attempts to change your mind about yourself.

Jesus is telling us that he has placed great emphasis on this idea, which should be a red flag to us signaling its crucial importance. Thus it is very important to take time to understand what this concept is all about. The world is an idea, as Schopenhauer stated over 150 years ago, although he did not conceive of its guilt-laden origin. The world is an idea that has never left its source in the mind. If it has not left its source in the mind, it is not "out there." If it is not out there, why should I worry about it? Why should I try to change, fix, or save it? Why should I try to teach *A Course in Miracles* to it? Why should I preach the gospel of Jesus Christ to it? Why should I *do* anything? That, of course, is the point of the section entitled "I Need Do Nothing" in the text (T-18.VII).

We just need to remember that what needs to be changed is our minds, which contain only two thoughts: the thought of the ego—separation, guilt, and death; and the thought of the Holy Spirit—Atonement, forgiveness, and healing. Jesus' central message to us is that we are not a body but a mind. This is a key theme in the workbook, where we are repeatedly asked to remember: *"I am not a body. I am free. For I am still as God created me"* (W-pI.rVI.in.3:3-5). In fact, the statement, "I am as God created me," in addition to being repeated throughout workbook Review VI, appears three times as complete lessons: 94, 110, and 162. It is closely paraphrased or suggested in Lessons 237, 260, and 282, and is also found as a statement at the end of the text in T-31.VIII.5:2. Its continual appearance underscores its importance in the thought system Jesus is helping us to learn.

God created us as spirit, not body. However, it is not necessary to hit yourself over the head in an attempt to beat the concept into it. You do not, for example, have to put it on a tape and play it every night while you are sleeping. Just be aware that the statement is true, and bring your illusory thoughts about yourself and others to that truth. This is accomplished though monitoring your thoughts, trying not to tolerate the mind wandering through projection. Try not to indulge your ego by continually focusing your attention on your body, the world, and problems in the world, but gently forgiving yourself when you do.

It is my *mind* that I must change. What student of *A Course in Miracles* does not know this line by heart: "Therefore, seek not to change the world, but choose to change you mind about the world" (T-21.in.1:7)? This does not necessarily mean my body will not do things in the world. It might do a great deal that could be seen by others as helpful, and that even seem to change things in the world. If I am right-minded, however, I know that I am not a body doing anything. I could care less about what is going on "outside," because if I am focused within, I am learning to accept the Atonement for myself and then only love will infuse me; only love will be reflected in what my body says and does. My focus will not be on the *form* because my job is to stay with the *content*. As Jesus says: "Concern yourself not with the extension of holiness, for the nature of miracles you do not understand. Nor do you do them" (T-16.II.1:3-4). Our responsibility is to forgive, but how forgiveness extends through us is not our concern. What a relief once it is accepted!

The Extension of Love

Before continuing, let me comment a bit more about love and its extension. Love is our natural reality and is all there is. We do not have to be concerned about love or do anything about it, because it simply *is*. What we have to do, however, is remove the blocks to remembering its presence in our minds. Our *guilt* over killing God covers love; this guilt then becomes so terrifying that it is covered by the *world*, which successfully shields us from guilt because we now see it in everyone else. We think we are unhappy because of something someone else has done, not because we attacked God by separating from Him. We now can blame this someone for our unhappiness and problems.

What we have to do, therefore, is remove the two shields we have put up. The outer is the projection that says: "You are responsible for my misery and the misery of people I care about." To remove this shield, we have to recall the projection. That is when we ask for help to see that the problem is inside, not outside. Our attention thus turns away from those we have judged as evil, as we come to realize that our pain has been caused by our guilt, which we have chosen over love. This is how the first shield is removed, leaving our guilt over killing God in order to have life as an individual. That is all that remains to block out the love that is always present in our minds. Thus we learn from Jesus that, just as our anger was made up, so, too, was our guilt: a decision made to protect ourselves from love, in whose non-dualistic presence our individual, separated self must disappear.

Our responsibility is to ask for help: first, in turning away from the world's dream to the mind's secret dream of separation and guilt; second, to be able to look at the secret dream and realize it is not true. Once we have taken those two steps, the shields have been removed and the veils are gone. At that point love will simply extend through us, taking whatever form is helpful. We as individuals are totally irrelevant. The self we believe we are has done its part by getting itself out of love's way.

Again, I am not responsible for love, nor its extension. My responsibility is only to forgive, which I do by asking for help in taking those two steps. After that the barriers are gone. The love that is in me, as it is in everyone, simply flows through. It infuses my mind and guides my body to do and say whatever is helpful, in whatever form it would be experienced as helpful.

There is a pithy passage in Lesson 23 in the workbook (among many, many others throughout *A Course in Miracles*), in which Jesus says that the first two steps in the process are our responsibility. Those are the steps of first bringing the problem from the outside to the inside, and then realizing that the problem inside is one we made up. He concludes by saying the third step—which inevitably and automatically follows—is not our responsibility (W-pI.23.5).

As I mentioned earlier, Jesus emphasizes the importance of a *little* willingness. Our part is very small. This little willingness is what Jesus is referring to in the text when he says: "Your task is not to seek for love, but merely to seek and find all of the barriers within yourself that you have built against it" (T-16.IV.6:1). Love will take care of itself. Our job is to seek out those barriers with Jesus, and then to look at them with him, which means looking without judgment. We then come to realize that the choice for guilt has seemingly cast us out of the Kingdom. We have chosen a world of worms devouring worms—a world of hate, misery, suffering, and death—over a world of love. When we genuinely look on that, we should properly be nauseated. How could we have been so dumb? How could we still be so dumb and continue to believe such insanity? Again, our responsibility is to seek and find the barriers we have placed between ourselves and love, and to ask Jesus' help in looking at them with his eyes: without judging ourselves or anyone else. As we practice this forgiveness the barriers disappear, and what remains is love and its extension through us.

These barriers preventing our awareness of love's presence are guilt's projections; i.e., our special relationships. What removes them—undoing specialness—is the miracle, or forgiveness. What then remains, once again, is the Love of God, which will automatically guide us to do and say what is most helpful.

Helen was in the habit of asking Jesus for specific help, such as: "What should I say to this person?" She once received a message from Jesus in which he told her:

> You cannot ask, "What shall I say to him?" and hear God's answer. Rather ask instead, "Help me to see this brother through the eyes of truth and not of judgment," and the help of God and all His angels will respond (*Absence from Felicity*, p. 381).

This is a most important statement. In fact, one could safely say that it goes to the heart of what *A Course in Miracles* is all about. Jesus was saying to Helen, and to all of us: "Do not ask me to tell you what to do in the world. I do not care about an illusion, about a world that does not exist. Ask me instead to help you remove your judgments; the thoughts of guilt, hate, and death that are in your mind. *They* are the problem."

In order for Jesus to help us remove the barriers to love, we have first to look at them with him. We accomplish this by seeing their projections, because that is what we first experience. We are aware only of being angry, fearful, depressed, or in pain about someone or some situation in the world. If we let him, Jesus will direct our attention back to the mind, where we will find the thoughts that gave rise to these projections. So here again we see why *ideas leave not their source* is such an important concept. The ideas of anger, fear, depression, and pain have never left their source in our minds. That is where change must take place if change is to occur at all. Meaningful change can occur only at the *source*. That is how poor Hamlet missed the whole point—he did not know that his problems were solely in his mind. But we are all poor Hamlets who miss the point, because we are always focused on the external: the body's life and death, and everything in between. Jesus thus is saying to us: "Nothing physical is the problem. Go within, because *ideas leave not their source*."

Now we return to Lesson 167:

"There is one life and that I share with God"—II

(3:8-11) It [*ideas leave not their source*] **is the reason you can heal. It is the cause of healing. It is why you cannot die. Its truth established you as one with God.**

When I return my attention to my mind I am at last addressing the problem. That is why I can heal. What has to be healed is not a broken bone, psyche, or peace treaty. What has to be healed is the mind that chose the ego and *thinks* there is a broken bone, psyche, or peace treaty, or anything else it perceives as requiring healing. That does not mean that a physician would not fix a broken bone, a therapist would not heal a wounded psyche, or a diplomat would not effect a peace treaty. But if these things were done from the right mind, the helpers would realize they were not the ones doing anything, because they would have met their one responsibility of choosing against the ego. They would have corrected the *cause* of the problem, which then allowed the love of Jesus in their right minds to work through their skills as a physician, therapist, or diplomat.

The reason Jesus says you cannot die is that the principle *ideas leave not their source* works not only for the ego's illusions, but for God's truth as well. If I am an idea in the Mind of God, and God is eternal and I am one with Him, I am eternal, too. That is why I cannot die. This naturally has nothing to do with the body, for Jesus is not saying your body can live forever. Whether or not you live for a long time is not the point at all. Rather, Jesus is saying that life is of the mind, which has been obscured by the thought of death, which is also in the mind.

(4:1) Death is the thought that you are separate from your Creator.

We have already looked at the idea that we became separate from our Creator when we brought death into the picture and believed we had killed our Source. The bottom line is that separation cannot exist in the presence of oneness. Within the insane dream, as long as we believe we are separate individuals oneness has been obliterated. *That* is the thought of death, and the very idea of *self* symbolizes that thought.

(4:1-2) Death is the thought that you are separate from your Creator. It is the belief conditions change, emotions alternate because of causes you cannot control, you did not make, and you can never change.

This is where we end up: in a body and world where everything changes, including our emotions, and where we are forever victims of circumstances beyond our control. I may be happy, and then something happens outside me, for which I am not responsible and which I cannot

71

control. Now I am sad. The weather changes so that it is not to my advantage, as I perceive my advantage to be. Where I was happy before, now I am not. All that is certain is I am not responsible, and because I cannot control what is outside me, my emotional situation can never truly change. That hopelessness abounds in the world. Even when there are glimmers of hope, they are squelched because nothing ever truly works here. The world was made so that things would *not* work, at least not for long. The only true value of the world and body is that they become mirrors reflecting back to us a decision that we made in our minds.

(4:3) It is the fixed belief ideas can leave their source, and take on qualities the source does not contain, becoming different from their own origin, apart from it in kind as well as distance, time and form.

Death says the Son of God has left his Source and become Its exact opposite. As we have already seen, that is the origin of the world of opposites: the original thought of opposition to God when we established ourselves as separate from Him. Life *and* death now reigned supreme as the law of nature, with the body replacing spirit as the Son's reality, and the ego replacing God as Creator.

"The Attraction of Death"

Now we will turn to the third obstacle to peace, "The Attraction of Death" (T-19.IV-C) The first two obstacles are "The Attraction of Guilt" (T-19.IV-A.i) and "The Attraction of Pain" (T-19.IV-B.i). As I said earlier, this is not the *fear* of death, but the *attraction* to it. The ego is attracted to death because, as we have seen, what the ego regards as life depends upon the idea of death. While our conscious selves may fear the body's end, our unconscious ego minds luxuriate in the thought, for death means life, and life means separation.

It is important to keep in mind that the ego in us is not a separate entity. It is not a thing, nor the devil. It is not anything other than the part of our minds that likes being us and enjoys being on its own—independent, separated, and special. It is that thought, incidentally, that is the basis of everyone's authority problem (T-3.VI), often expressed by our not appreciating being told what to do, think, or believe. The fact that we have an authority problem does not mean, by the way, that we can resolve it by becoming automatons. We are not asked by the Holy Spirit to always do what authorities tell us. Many times that would not be a wise nor loving thing to do.

The authority problem as discussed in *A Course in Miracles* is about our *attitude*, which often is experienced as a quick stiffening or resistance in the presence of an authority who tells us something, whether it is something trivial or important. It is not necessarily about our behavior in doing or not doing what an authority tells us. Our reaction may be communicating to us, quoting Hamlet: *"Something is rotten in the state of Denmark"* (I,iv,90). And there is indeed something rotten going on, but it is in our minds: the guilt over our original authority problem with God. We are thus asked to accept the authority of the Holy Spirit rather than the authority of the ego, which always thinks in terms of specialness, whether in rebellion or obedience.

"Who is the author of my reality, God or the ego?" That is the question posed in the original authority problem, and in our insanity we believe we are locked in a struggle with our Creator, Whom we believe is fighting us for control of our lives. The authority problem is why, among other reasons, we scripted into our lives a period called adolescence. That is one of the most god-awful things the ego ever imagined for us, and the authority problem is expressed in what we call the "adolescent rebellion," when adolescents define themselves in opposition to their parents. This takes the form of statements such as: "You don't understand me!" "Let me do what I want!" "Allow me to be creative." "You don't trust me." "You don't give me enough freedom." And on and on and on. We have all lived through that stage, and we *still* live through it, because it reflects what is in our minds, exactly what we acted out with God. On the other end, when authorities do not feel secure within themselves in the presence of opposition, they often become hardened, rigid, punitive, and abusive. That happens between parents and children, teachers and students, and on the national and international levels as well.

As long as the authority problem is present in our minds, it will inevitably be acted out in our lives. It is in the infant who learns the word *no*—"No one is going to tell me what to do!" Unfortunately, the adolescent rebellion does not end at the age of twenty or twenty-one, nor does it have its roots in the "terrible twos." It goes back to the original projection in our minds when we believed God wanted to control us.

And unless we resolve that fundamental issue in our minds, we—personally and collectively—will continue to act out our authority problem in the world.

God does *not* want to control us. That is the ego's idea of God, not the true God. There is no control in Heaven. How can there be? There is no one to control and no one to be controlled. There is only One. Control has meaning only in a dualistic universe, which is a universe of death, because the one who is in control seeks to retain control and believes he will die unless he has it. And the one who feels he is being controlled believes it is a life-or-death issue. We are always struggling with the same life-or-death issues. We are attracted to death because—as I was explaining earlier—death proves that we have life. If we have life, then sin and guilt are real, punishment is justified, and the separation becomes a real event in our awareness. That is why, in the third obstacle to peace, Jesus speaks of the *attraction* of death. It is our mind's attraction to the ego's thought system of separation.

Let us, then, look at this third obstacle, beginning with paragraph 1, sentence 4:

(T-19.IV-C.1:4-5) No one can die unless he chooses death. What seems to be the fear of death is really its attraction.

Jesus likes this idea so much that in the workbook he repeats it using somewhat different words: "And no one dies without his own consent" (W-pI.152.1:4). "No one can die unless he chooses death." Why would you choose it unless you wanted it? And if you want it, obviously it is attractive to you and serves a purpose.

The one who chooses death is not the one who seems to be dying. Bodies do not choose, any more than bodies die. The choice is made in the mind, where the choice is made to be born into a body and subjected to the body's laws. We die, not because of nature's law that bodies die, but because we have chosen to identify with the thought system that wants death to be real. If you toss a coin into the air and it falls to the ground, it is not because of the law of gravity. There *is* no law of gravity, except in dreams. Your mind decided to make a world in which there is a law of gravity, and your mind made a decision to live in that world under its laws. That is why the coin falls when you drop it. That is why, when Galileo did his famous experiment, the objects fell from the top of the Tower of Pisa. It had nothing to do with the so-called law of gravity.

This point is very important. *There are no laws in this world.* How could nothing have a law? How could a lifeless piece of wood that we dress up to look like something, but we know is a puppet, do anything independently? The mind made up a body and a world to be governed by laws that *seem* real and external to the mind that made them up. Why? Because *we wanted to forget why and how we came here.* We wanted to forget our minds so all we would be aware of would be our bodies, living in a world under its laws. This was all a trick on the part of the ego, an ingenious magician and brilliant general orchestrating a clandestine war against God, which is really a war against us. This hidden desire, the ego's secret wish, is what Jesus points to when he extends his previous statement about the world being an outside picture of an inward condition. Near the end of Chapter 24 he teaches us: "[Perception] is the outward picture of a wish; an image that you wanted to be true" (T-24.VII.8:10). The law of gravity, and all the other laws of the world hold because we *want* them to hold.

We—the decision maker in our minds—are the ones who govern what goes on here. That is why there are certain people who appear to transcend the laws of the world—who seem to be able to defy the law of gravity and levitate, or who can stay under water for thirty minutes. All they do is go to the place in their minds that subscribes to these laws, and then change their minds about them. That does not necessarily mean that they are spiritually advanced people, although some might be. They are able to get back to their minds, but that does not necessarily mean their *right* minds. It does mean, though, that they understand the mind's power. That could be helpful, but could also be abused. It is all too easy to form a special relationship with that power, repeating what we all did at the beginning when we accused ourselves of stealing power from God to use for our own selfish advantage.

Sometimes people are afraid to do anything with their minds because they fear they will misuse that power again. Of course, once they believe that, they are caught. If you fear misusing the power again, you have already done so in your mind, which goes directly against the principle of the Atonement that says there was no abuse; nothing happened: "Not one note in Heaven's song was missed" (T-26.V.5:4). However, many people are so guilty over that imagined abuse that they choose to be ineffectual in this world, keeping themselves even more out of touch with their minds. However, guilt and fear are easily undone once we accept Jesus' help in getting back within, so that we can gently look with him at what is *seemingly* there, so we may look beyond to what is *really* there.

A major objective of the workbook—the practical application of the text—is to help us realize our minds are split. Our collective mind made the world and body, but our minds are split between the wrong-minded home of the ego and the right-minded home of the Holy Spirit, and we can choose with which mind we will identify. The purpose of the workbook, then, is to have us realize that we have a mind and a choice. The mind training that Jesus teaches involves our realizing, first, that we have a mind and that it is our thoughts that make our world; and second, that our minds can choose to follow either the ego or the Holy Spirit.

That learning is the essence of *A Course in Miracles*. Once we accept its basic principle we can go through our lives, day in and day out, asking for help to see how our minds determine our reactions. We are never upset for the reason we think, as we are taught in Lesson 5 (W-pI.5). Our anger is never justified because nothing out there has the power to upset us, cause us pain, or kill us. The body can be killed, but we are not bodies. A passage in the text says: "Are thoughts, then, dangerous? To bodies, yes! The thoughts that seem to kill are those that teach the thinker that he *can* be killed" (T-21.VIII.1:1-3). Thus the major thrust of our learning is that we are not bodies, but minds.

Before you can learn that you are spirit and have never left home, you first have to learn that you are a mind that harbors thoughts of hate and death, along with thoughts of love and peace. You have to learn you can choose between these two thoughts, and that that choice determines how you perceive the world, which then determines how you respond to it: with love and kindness, or with fear, anxiety, and projection. As your learning progresses, death becomes less and less of an issue, because you will know more and more that death is a thought. You learn that you can do relatively little about the world or the body, but you can certainly do a great deal about your thoughts.

That is why *A Course in Miracles* offers us genuine hope. It gets to the source of the problem, and offers us the means of doing something about it. This means we need to move beyond all questions that but reflect our belief the ego is true, alive, and well. Think how much different the meaning of Hamlet's soliloquy would have been if he had said: "To be, or not to be: that is *not* the question." It would have destroyed the meter, but its meaning would have changed the course of our hero's life.

(1:5-8) What seems to be the fear of death is really its attraction. Guilt, too, is feared and fearful. Yet it could have no hold at all except on those who are attracted to it and seek it out. And so it is with death.

Death and guilt would have no hold on us unless we wanted them to. Our problem is not that our bodies get older, deteriorate, and die. Our problem is *the thought that wants* our bodies to get older, deteriorate, and die. Physical changes leading to death "prove" that changelessness is not reality. Change and death "prove" that true life is a myth. It does not seem this way to us because we are out of touch with our minds. We think our minds are our brains. Thus we need a Teacher who continually reminds us that we are mind, and that *ideas leave not their source.* The idea that we are physical and psychological beings is an idea of separation that has never left its source in our minds.

The purpose of *A Course in Miracles* is to bring us back to our minds where we truly are. We are the dreamer, not the dream: "The miracle establishes you dream a dream, and that its content is not true" (T-28.II.7:1). I am not a figure in the dream, I am the dreamer of the dream. I am the mind who dreams of a world filled with separate bodies, including what I consider to be my own. The theme of this dreaming is a tale of guilt, fear, death, punishment, and suffering—all of which, being of the dream, is not true. It is my dream, but that cannot make it my reality. All salvation requires is that I recognize it is *my* dream, not the world's. Certainly, it is everyone's dream. But all I need focus on is my part in it, a part I have chosen. In other words, I *want* to be upset by thoughts of death and loss, thoughts of rejection, abandonment, infidelity, poverty, and sickness. My dream can have no hold on me except as I am attracted to it and seek it out. None of these things— guilt, death, abandonment, pain, etc.—can affect me unless I am first attracted to them and seek them out. As Jesus says in the text: "Let them [the figures in the dream] be as hateful and as vicious as they may, they could have no effect on you unless you failed to recognize it is your dream" (T-27.VIII.10:6).

The one who is attracted to this thought system of guilt and pain, however, is not the self I think I am. It is the puppeteer who controls that self who is so attracted: the decision-making part of my mind that wants to remain an ego. Realizing this means for the first time in my life I am becoming aware I have a mind. That is what *A Course in*

Miracles does for us: it teaches us we have a mind. That is why understanding its theory is so important. Not that such understanding is healing in and of itself, but it provides a context in which we can begin to understand what is going on in our lives: why nothing has ever worked; why we are up one day and down the next; why our love and peace are not constant, and why they appear to be taken from us instantaneously.

We want to live a life of change because that is what proves the opposite of changelessness is true, which means changelessness is false. If death is the opposite of life, and death is real, then life in Heaven must be an illusion. Eternal life and death cannot coexist. The ego tries to blend life and death, just as it tries to blend love and hate, but they are mutually exclusive states. Real love cannot coexist with hate, and true life cannot coexist with death. Special love can coexist with special hate, because they are actually the same. The body's life can coexist with physical death, because they, too, are ultimately the same. But real love and real life do not have an opposite. That is why we speak of *A Course in Miracles* as an uncompromising non-dualistic system.

(1:8-9) And so it is with death. Made by the ego, its [guilt's] **dark shadow falls across all living things, because the ego is the "enemy" of life.**

Remember, this is about death as a thought, made by the ego in the original unholy instant when we believed we separated from God and destroyed Him. That is why thoughts of death are so painful and repugnant to us. They remind us of that original thought, which is so fraught with guilt there seems no way we could ever approach it. Projection is the reason, as we are continually impelled to get rid of the guilt, but can never do so because *ideas leave not their source.* The guilt always remains with us.

Think of poor Lady Macbeth! Her guilt over the murder of King Duncan caused her to imagine she still had his blood on her hands. There was no blood, of course, because she had washed it off; but she continued to see it and pathetically laments: *"All the perfumes of Arabia will not sweeten this little hand"* (V,i,50). Like Hamlet, Lady Macbeth is everyone, for we can never wash the guilt from our minds: *ideas leave not their source.* Incidentally, a reference to Lady Macbeth's predicament is found in the manual for teachers:

> Kill or be killed, for here alone is choice. Beyond this there is none, for what was done cannot be done without. The stain of blood can never be removed, and anyone who bears this stain on him must meet with death (M-17.7:11-13).

Lady Macbeth's compulsive hand washing symbolizes our need to project. We want to expunge our guilt by projecting it out, but the "stain of blood" never leaves. It continually returns because it never left: Again: *Ideas leave not their source.* Thus are we compelled continually to project, in the magical hope that our guilt will be undone. Freud's concept of *repetition compulsion* can be understood in this sense, as we are compelled to repeat the same neurotic pattern over and over. But the pattern will never change until we undo its cause: the decision in our minds to ally with the ego instead of with the Holy Spirit.

To repeat: "Made by the ego, its [death's] dark shadow falls across all living things, because the ego is the 'enemy' of life." The ego's "life" was born from death, and death is the enemy of life. Our guilt over the thought we could extract life from the death of God is continually being projected into the world. But bodies do not have life, and there are no true laws that govern the life of the body. This is what Jesus means in saying that we are under no laws but God's (W-pI.76). He is not encouraging us to flout the laws of the body and the world. He is simply saying we should be aware the body's laws do not truly exist. We chose to believe in the laws of the body and the world so that we would always be struggling with them, to be distracted from ever realizing their source was a thought in our minds, let alone remembering that we *are* mind. But Jesus tells us in the first lines of Lesson 158:

> What has been given you? The knowledge that you are a mind, in Mind and purely mind, sinless forever, wholly unafraid, because you were created out of Love. Nor have you left your Source, remaining as you were created (W-pI.158.1:1-3).

In summary: Bodies do not die because bodies do not live. They have no life. Bodies die only in our dream where they are a projection of the thought of death, and it is that thought that has to be changed if we are truly going to live.

(2:1) And yet a shadow cannot kill.

A shadow is nothing. It is simply the absence of light, caused by an interference or block. Similarly, the body does not die because of a biological law that says bodies must die. The body simply has the *appearance* of death, because the thought of death in the mind dictates it. It is that thought that is the interference to our remembering the thought of life, and so it is that thought that must be removed.

To repeat an earlier point: We are not under the laws of gravity, health, death, and birth. We are the source of those laws insofar as the decision-making part of our minds chose them when it chose to identify with the ego thought system. In that sense, we placed ourselves under the laws of guilt and death. And since it was our dream to do so—*our* wish to remain separated—we have the power to awaken from it.

(2:2-3) What is a shadow to the living? They but walk past and it is gone.

Thus, you walk outside on a sunny day and see a shadow of a tree. You just walk through it. There is nothing to stop you. It has no effect on you because it is nothing. Again, it is but the absence of light, and has no substance of itself. It remains a shadow.

(2:4) But what of those whose dedication is not to live; the black-draped "sinners," the ego's mournful chorus [i.e., the parade of bodies that have walked across the stage we call life]**, plodding so heavily away from life, dragging their chains and marching in the slow procession that honors their grim master, lord of death?**

The ego is "lord of death" because it is the thought of death. Strictly speaking, it is the decision-making part of our minds that is the true lord, since it alone has the power to choose life or death, God or the ego.

(2:5) Touch any one of them with the gentle hands of forgiveness, and watch the chains fall away, along with yours.

Jesus is saying that what would finally motivate you to decide you no longer want these chains is realizing that death is a thought you have chosen because you wanted to preserve your individual identity, and you now recognize it is not worth the price. You realize your choice for the ego has only brought you grief, sadness, and pain, for it excluded you from the Love of God. You realize at last it is that Love you want above all else, and that this Love has nothing to do with the world.

Choosing against the thought of individuality and death, you change your perception of the body and the world, now seen for the shadows they truly are. Thus, "touch any one of them with the gentle hands of forgiveness," and the chains of guilt, fear, death, grief, sadness and pain fall away. Note that the hands are *gentle*, reflecting the process of forgiveness that entails *only* looking at our mistaken choice without judgment. Nothing more is asked of us. Recall our discussion how love opposes nothing. Therefore the ego need not be opposed, simply looked at without judgment, and "touched with the gentle hands of forgiveness."

Skip down to sentence 12, where Jesus tells us what happens when we have made these changes:

(2:12) Your dedication is not to death, nor to its master.

Rather than dedicating ourselves to the ego, the master that dictates death, we have now changed our allegiance so that our dedication is no longer "to death or to its master," but to life and its Teacher.

(2:13) When you accepted the Holy Spirit's purpose in place of the ego's you renounced death, exchanging it for life.

Once again, this is not about anything external; not about the body but about thought. The ego's purpose is to prove separation real by proving that sin, guilt, punishment, and death are real. Thus it makes up a world that gives seeming witness to the reality of these ideas. We are ready to change our purpose when we can sincerely say: "I do not want this anymore. There must be another way, for the pain is too great. I have exhausted every possibility, and nothing works." We may even realize that *A Course in Miracles* does not work the way we have used it, because we employed it to make the body's dream real. Now we see we made *our* course to underlay Jesus' Course. Now we choose to follow a different master: the Master of Life instead of death. Thus we refocus our attention from the body to the mind—not through death, but through the shift of perception Jesus calls the miracle.

(2:14-15) We know that an idea leaves not its source. And death is the result of the thought we call the ego, as surely as life is the result of the Thought of God.

Once again Jesus is making it abundantly clear that *A Course in Miracles* has nothing to do with the body; nothing to do with anything external. We are talking only about thought because there *is* only thought. If *ideas leave not their source*, then the ideas of guilt and death cannot leave their source in our minds, to be projected out as the embodiment of the thought of separation. If *ideas leave not their source*, then the thought of separation cannot make a real body and world outside our minds.

Our understanding becomes crystal clear, for decision now is simplified. Everything is either the thought of the ego—the thought of death—or the thought of the Holy Spirit—the thought of life. Our choices as well are now clear. We go through our days knowing that each and every time we have an ego response we can look at it with Jesus, realizing we can make another choice. As we practice, we become increasingly adept at noticing such ego responses as mild irritation, depression, sadness, anger, anxiety, and special love attachments.

As we become more aware, we can stop ourselves almost as quickly as we have the thought and realize: "I have chosen the wrong master again. I have chosen the lord of death instead of the Lord of Life." Maybe I will want to continue on that path for the moment, but at least I know what I am doing. I understand I have chosen the ego instead of the Holy Spirit because I am afraid of His Love, fearful that if I take Jesus' hand I will walk with him out of the dream, marking the end of my individual self. *That* is my fear. With this new awareness I recognize the symptoms of anxiety, depression, anger, or specialness as being but the outside pictures of an inward decision, and one I can change whenever I wish.

This is all extraordinarily helpful, and we are not asked to do anything else. We are not asked to change our decisions. We are not asked to change our feelings or give up our specialness. We are simply asked to look honestly at our egos. It is the looking without judgment that will weaken our identification with the ego. That is very important. That is why Jesus says: "This course requires almost nothing of you. It is impossible to imagine one that asks so little, or could offer more" (T-20.VII.1:7-8). He is not asking us to change our egos or give up anything at all, but only to change our inner teacher. Thus will we be replacing an angry, guilt-ridden, depressed self with a self that becomes increasingly joyful, peaceful, and happy, regardless of external circumstances. This all hinges on the principle, *ideas leave not their source*. The problem is the *source*, not the projected form of the *idea*.

Skip now to paragraph 5, sentence 2:

(5:2-5) The body no more dies than it can feel. It does nothing. Of itself it is neither corruptible nor incorruptible. It *is* nothing.

Nothing happens to the body. It does not change, nor is it made to be unholy or holy. It *does* nothing, for it *is* nothing.

(5:6) It is the result of a tiny, mad idea of corruption that can be corrected.

Corruption here is meant in the sense of a change that results in deterioration—because the ego is a corrupted thought, a distorted thought that states I am a Son of God who is independent and separate from his Source. That is the corruption that results in the ego's travesty of the Self that God created:

> What is this son that you have made to be your strength? What is this child of earth on whom such love is lavished? What is this parody of God's creation that takes the place of yours? (T-24.VII.1:9-11)

Again: "The body no more dies than it can feel. It does nothing. Of itself it is neither corruptible nor incorruptible. It *is* nothing. It is the result of a tiny, mad idea of corruption that can be corrected." It is helpful to keep lines like these in mind as you go through your day, aware of how your attention is centered on your body as well as other people's bodies. You do not have to change your focus; just be aware of how you *want* your attention to be riveted outside your mind, in order to avoid the possibility of changing it.

Move to paragraph 11:

(11:1) When anything seems to you to be a source of fear ...

Jesus is speaking to us here the same way he does in the workbook: "Pay attention, be vigilant throughout your day to anything that upsets you, and then ask me for help. Bring the darkness of your illusory thoughts and feelings to the light of my truth."

(11:1) When anything seems to you to be a source of fear, when any situation strikes you with terror and makes your body tremble and the cold sweat of fear comes over it, remember it is always for *one* reason; the ego has perceived it as a symbol of fear, a sign of sin and death.

The ego has taken the thoughts of sin and death and made them real to us, rooted in our very identity as a separated entity. After making them real, the ego then tells us: "These are so horrible you must never look at them. Therefore, you must project these thoughts from your mind into the world."

Any time something in the world upsets us, it is because we have listened to the ego that tells us not look within at the thoughts of fear, sin, and death. "Do not look within," the ego says, "look to the world, and let me help you deal with the problems you perceive there." This is the background for the passages in Chapter 2 of the text, when Helen complained to Jesus about some fear, and he said to her:

> ... you cannot ask me to release you from fear. [I cannot do that.] You should ask, instead, for help in the conditions that have brought the fear about. These conditions always entail a willingness to be separate (T-2.VII.1:2; T-2.VI.4:3-4).

That is exactly what he is saying in Chapter 19 about the attraction of death, except that here he is saying it more poetically.

Still in Chapter 2, Jesus continues to advise Helen:

> If I intervened between your thoughts and their results [in other words, if I did not respect your mind's decision to be separate], I would be tampering with a basic law of cause and effect; the most fundamental law there is. I would hardly help you if I depreciated the power of your own thinking. This would be in direct opposition to the purpose of this course (T-2.VII.1:4-6).

It was very early in the scribing when Jesus said this to Helen, and it is interesting to note how even at the beginning he was emphasizing the Course's purpose of teaching us the power of our minds and the inherent powerlessness of the world: How can the non-existent have power? Likewise, how can the body's laws have power? All power but rests in the mind of the dreamer that makes the world, and then forgets its part. Thus Jesus is teaching us here that whenever we get upset we should remember that what upsets us is a symbol of a thought that is in our own mind.

Now comes an extremely important statement:

(11:2) Remember, then, that neither sign nor symbol should be confused with source, for they must stand for something other than themselves.

Jesus is telling us: "Do not make the error real by making the world real, confusing symbol with source. Do not believe you are afraid because of an external situation, which is only a symbol of your fear. What you are truly afraid of is the source: your mind's decision to be separate. It is *that* decision, and its concomitant guilt, that produces the fear."

He talks about this same idea later in the text: "This is a course in cause and not effect" (T-21.VII.7:8). This is a course about the *mind*: the source and cause. It is not about effects: the world, body, and external events—all symbols of the thought of separation. *A Course in Miracles* will restore to your awareness the power of your mind— source, cause—to choose. Jesus is not interested in the *effects* of your mistaken choice, because they have never left their *cause* and remain one with it: *ideas leave not their source*; effects leave not their cause, and but represent either a thought of fear and death, or a thought of love and forgiveness. Everything in this world stands for one of these two thoughts.

(11:3) Their meaning cannot lie in them, but must be sought in what they represent.

Meaning is not *in* symbols, and cannot be found in forms, bodies, or objects. You must go back to the symbol's origin, which is where change occurs, as we saw in Lesson 167.

(11:4) And they may thus mean everything or nothing, according to the truth or falsity of the idea which they reflect.

The meaning here is quite clear: What alone is important is the idea of Atonement or separation, life or death, forgiveness or attack. We are always trying to understand the meaning of events in this world; but their *meaning* does not lie in the events themselves, which is why no one truly understands anything here. We can understand them only when we get to their source, which is the mind's decision. What seems external is simply a symbol of that decision. "And they may thus mean everything or nothing, according to the truth or falsity of the idea which they reflect."

This is why the early workbook lessons emphasize that our thoughts about what we see mean nothing. They are meaningless because they come from the ego and therefore represent a point of view that says separation is real, and therefore what we perceive outside and separate from us is real as well. What gives our perceived objects true meaning is realizing they have not left their source in the mind. What we see outside is a projection of what we have made real inside: separation or unity, differences or sameness, judgment or vision. The source of those two meanings lies within.

You will know the idea the projections reflect—the ego or the Holy Spirit—by your reaction. Anything that disturbs your peace, leads to a perception of differences (not the superficial differences on the level of form) that you think really make a difference, or causes you to perceive the Sonship of God as anything but a perfect unity—*must* come from the ego, a thought of separation, fear, and death. The thought itself emanated from the original perception of differences. Expressed in story form, we could say that there was originally God and His Son, who no longer liked his Father. He stole his Father's treasure and established his own kingdom of separation and fragmentation. From that point on, the Son, now Sons, believed everyone else was going to do to them exactly what they accused themselves of doing to God. They believed others would steal from them, but they really accuse themselves of having stolen first.

That is how we all came to be: we stole. Everyone is a closet kleptomaniac, and we cannot help ourselves. That is why it is most helpful to be vigilant about our reactions, paying careful attention to our perceptions of the world around us. The world is a mirror—what Freud referred to as the "royal road"—that leads us back to the decision-making process in our minds.

Chapter 4

DEATH FROM THE PERSPECTIVE
OF THE HEALED MIND

Up to this point I have been focusing almost exclusively on the thought of death, which gave rise to the fear of death with all its ramifications. But there is also a thought of truth, or life. When we identify with that thought we perceive everything in the world differently. This does not mean that the external world will be any different, or that bodies will not physically die. It simply means that when our perceptions are healed, and we have chosen to identify with the thought of life rather than the thought of death—the thought of sameness and unity instead of the thought of differences and separation—we will *perceive* death in an entirely different way; not as punishment for sin, not as anything tragic. To the contrary, we shall not see death as anything at all.

When you accept the thought of life you will look in the same way on any form of fear and death: a death camp, AIDS, the West Nile virus, or an impending or ongoing war. Your eyes will see what everyone else sees, but your mind will interpret it differently because you will be coming from a different source: a thought of life or Atonement that says the separation never occurred. Therefore there is no sin or guilt, and therefore no reason to fear punishment. *There is no death*, which simply means there is no body. The body is nothing other than the embodiment of the thoughts of sin, guilt, fear, death, separation, differences, and opposites. And so when you identify with the Holy Spirit's thought of Atonement, although your eyes see like everyone else, your *interpretation* and *reaction* will be totally different. You will realize that "frightened people can be vicious" (T-3.I.4:2). Needless to say, viciousness abounds in our world, but its underlying thought of fear is only a cover for the thought of love. When fear is projected it becomes a thought of hate: "I am afraid I will be attacked, therefore I will attack first. I have to be vicious and cruel, because I am surrounded by evil people who would do terrible things to me if I let them." When I am not in touch with my guilt, I have no way of realizing that what I am accusing others of is what I am secretly accusing myself of.

Hamlet was not aware his accusations against his uncle and mother were an indictment of himself. If he had, he would not have made the judgments he did, and would not have seen death as punishment. Rather, he would have seen death as a simple laying down of the body. The one place in the Course material that speaks of death this way comes in *The Song of Prayer*, the section called "False versus True Healing." The term *false healing* refers to our attempts to heal the symbol—the body—instead of *true healing*, which undoes through forgiveness what the symbol represents: the thought of separation and guilt.

We begin with paragraph 1, sentence 8:

(S-3.II.1:8) Yet there is a kind of seeming death that has a different source.

Jesus will now speak of death from the perspective of one whose mind is healed. The word *seeming* is used here because there really is no death.

(1:9) It does not come because of hurtful thoughts and raging anger at the universe.

One could also say, raging anger *from* the universe. There is a widely known story of Beethoven's death, the veracity of which will never be ascertained, although it is certainly characteristic of the tempestuous titan. At the moment of his death there was a clap of thunder, and the great composer is said to have raised himself from the bed, shaking his fist at the heavens. One could see that as an expression of "raging anger at the universe": "You will not triumph over me!"

But when your mind is healed, death "does not come because of hurtful thoughts and raging anger at the universe."

(1:10) It merely signifies the end has come for usefulness of body functioning.

Your body was but a classroom in which you learned the lessons of forgiveness. Once you did so, the body became the means of having forgiveness taught *through you*. You did not teach; the teaching came *through you* automatically. Without any impediments in your mind, the love within you—the Atonement principle—flowed without effort, concern, or thought on your part, gently guiding your words and behavior. Everything you said or did automatically reflected the love with which you chose to identify.

(1:11) And so it is discarded as a choice, as one lays by a garment now outworn.

So death is no different from looking in your closet at some clothing—a suit, blouse, skirt, trousers, or whatever—and saying: "These are worn out; they have served me well, but I do not need them any more." And you would not give it another thought. That is all that death—the laying down of the body—would be from a right-minded perspective. Since your mind would be healed, there would be no thought of sin and fear, which would mean that you were no longer identified with your body. Those who still believed they were in the world would perceive your body as dying, but you—your mind—would know that that body was not you. Your identification would no longer be with the body and its thought system of sin and death, but with the thought system of the Atonement. Your mind healed, you would realize, therefore, that nothing was being done to nothing.

(2:1) This is what death should be; a quiet choice, made joyfully and with a sense of peace, because the body has been kindly used to help the Son of God along the way he goes to God.

The body has simply been an instrument for your learning. Once you have learned the lesson, the body becomes an instrument for the inner Teacher—the loving Thought we call the Holy Spirit—to teach through you, as we just saw. It becomes a "means of communication" (T-6.V-A.5:5). Rather than a means of separation and crucifixion, the body now is a way to symbolize the love that is present in all minds, which are in truth joined as one.

(2:2) We thank the body, then, for all the service it has given us.

This does not mean that we literally thank the body, because we would know there is no body to thank. Instead, the body now represents a correction for the hatred we had displaced onto our bodies—what our old friend Hamlet, and still older friends the Gnostics did. Remember, we hate the body when it becomes the repository of what we hate in ourselves. When we realize there is nothing to hate, guilt is gone and the body is recognized as nothing. There is nothing about it to be grateful for, and nothing *not* to be grateful for; nothing to hate and nothing to cherish. And for this understanding we are truly grateful.

(2:3-4) But we are thankful, too, the need is done to walk the world of limits, and to reach the Christ in hidden forms and clearly seen at most in lovely flashes. Now we can behold Him without blinders, in the light that we have learned to look upon again.

True perception, the vision of Christ, is now constant. The body had been a way of blocking vision, making the separation from one another seem real and palpable. But when the need to be separate is gone, the body no longer serves that function and the light of the Holy Spirit's Love can shine freely in our minds. The vision of Christ, which sees everyone as one, now becomes our only means of perception.

(3:1) We call it death, but it is liberty.

The meaning here is significantly different from the meaning of the line I quoted earlier: "There is a risk of thinking death is peace...." (T-27.VII.10:2). There Jesus was referring to our mistake of making the error real whenever we judge the world to be disgusting and repulsive, and whenever we find living here so painful that we want to be freed from it. That is *not* what he is speaking about in this passage. It would be impossible to perceive the world as disgusting or repulsive if there were no guilt in our minds. *Guilt* is what is so disgusting to us, not physical life. The *thought* of what we think we did in separating from God, and the *thought* that we continue to separate, are repulsive. Making the error real is what Jesus refers to in the text when he says: "Who punishes the body is insane" (T-28.VI.1:1). There is nothing to punish the body for. The body is nothing. It is the *thought* about which we are so guilty, again, that we find so disgusting and repulsive.

(3:2) It does not come in forms that seem to be thrust down in pain upon unwilling flesh, but as a gentle welcome to release.

Death is not something that comes unbidden, and attacks us from outside. Death is something that we choose. But our choice can be guided by the ego or the Holy Spirit. If we are guided by the ego, then we want to die so that we can blame someone—whether living or dead—and say to that person: "Behold me, brother [sister, father, mother, son, daughter—it does not matter who], at your hand I die" (T-27.I.4:6). But if we choose to be guided by the Holy Spirit, then death is a quiet letting go of nothing: "a gentle welcome to release."

(3:3-4) If there has been true healing, this can be the form in which death comes when it is time to rest a while from labor gladly done and gladly ended. Now we go in peace to freer air and gentler climate, where it is not hard to see the gifts we gave were saved for us.

This should not be taken literally. Jesus is saying that there is nothing to fear after death. Hamlet's apprehension about *"what dreams may come"* after death is not warranted. The concern is gone because the guilt is gone. When your mind is truly healed, as we have stated over and over, there is no guilt. That means there is no reason to project fear of punishment, whether in sickness, suffering, and death, or the period after death. The dreams that come after your mind is healed are happy dreams. Then we recognize that the gift of forgiveness we gave has been given us.

(3:5-4:1) For Christ is clearer now; His vision more sustained in us; His Voice, the Word of God, more certainly our own.
This gentle passage to a higher prayer, a kind forgiveness of the ways of earth, can only be received with thankfulness.

We do not have to be afraid of death, because we no longer perceive ourselves as bodies, and for this recognition we are grateful, as we are for the loving and gentle vision of unity we now enjoy.

(4:2) Yet first true healing must have come to bless the mind with loving pardon for the sins it dreamed about and laid upon the world.

Before you can have this peaceful death without guilt, you first have to do your homework. You have to look at the thoughts of sin you projected onto the world. That would be your focus, rather than death and what happens with your body. You do not have to do anything about those thoughts, except to pay attention to your projections onto others. That is how true healing occurs.

(4:3-4) Now are its dreams dispelled in quiet rest. Now its forgiveness comes to heal the world and it is ready to depart in peace, the journey over and the lessons learned.

The process of forgiveness, and indeed the process of healing, is the dispelling of dreams. This dispelling "in quiet rest" is a lovely description of the process. Without judging and hating, ranting and raving, kicking and screaming—but with the love of Jesus beside me—I look at my dreams. I look at my judgments, hates, and specialness—all the ways I have misused my body and everyone else's. I gently look, and am gently taught that what I see outside is coming from a decision I made in my mind. Thus does the world's dream quietly fall away, its place taken by the recognition of the secret dream, consisting of thoughts of judgment, fear, and specialness, preoccupation with the body—mine and other's—not to mention concern about problems in the world. I now realize all these came from my mind's decision to listen to the ego instead of the Holy Spirit. This quiet dispelling symbolizes the end of guilt, fear, anxiety, and judgment; the gentle looking with Jesus at the outer world of hate that allows me to see it as a projection of my inner world of hate, and one I no longer want.

(5:1-3) This is not death according to the world, for death is cruel in its frightened eyes and takes the form of punishment for sin. How could it be a blessing, then? And how could it be welcome when it must be feared?

We have already discussed the idea that the fear and discomfort surrounding death is the veil that conceals our deep-seated attraction to it.

(5:4-5) What healing has occurred in such a view of what is merely opening the gate to higher prayer and kindly justice done? Death is reward and not a punishment.

Death becomes reward in the sense that our learning from the Holy Spirit is over. The ending of the ego thought system is its own reward, and who would not greet the end of hell and the opening of Heaven's gate with anything but joy and gratitude? As Jesus states in the text:

> No one on earth but offers thanks to one who has restored his home, and sheltered him from bitter winter and the freezing cold. And shall the Lord of Heaven and His Son give less in gratitude for so much more? (T-26.IX.7:3-4)

(5:6) But such a viewpoint must be fostered by the healing that the world cannot conceive.

This is because the world conceives of healing as taking place externally, outside the mind. Thus our common perception is that there are external problems, symptoms, causes, and effects. But the healing that Jesus is teaching us is purely internal—the mind is the problem; the mind is the answer.

(5:7-8) There is no partial healing. What but shifts illusions has done nothing.

Healing is not accomplished by merely treating the symptom. True healing treats the cause, not the effect. Recall Freud's "symptom substitution," by which he meant the shift from one symptom to another that occurs when you do not undo the cause. The miracle, giving its name to our spiritual path, is the process of "giving back to cause the function of causation, not effect" (T-28.II.9:3). The miracle thus restores to the mind its power to cause effects, not to be the effect of an external cause. This true shift from effect to cause is the basis of all healing.

(5:9-11) What is false cannot be partly true. If you are healed your healing is complete. Forgiveness is the only gift you give and would receive.

This provides a criterion for understanding whether your forgiveness lessons have been learned—whether you have finally forgiven the world. Healing is complete to the extent you recognize the Sonship as complete. No one and nothing is left outside: "Not one illusion is accorded faith, and not one spot of darkness still remains to hide the face of Christ from anyone" (T-31.VIII.12:5). The love with which you identify, if it is true love, embraces the Sonship in its entirety, in forms that are animate or inanimate, pleasant or repulsive. You make no distinctions because there are no distinctions in God. That recognition is true healing.

Choosing to exclude certain aspects of the Sonship is a red flag alerting you that you have again chosen the ego, and so your healing is not complete. On a practical level you want to focus on whomever you wish to exclude at any given moment. That may be because you think someone else has something you lack, and so you want to cannibalize that person (special love); or because you have projected onto another the evil you think is in yourself, and therefore you seek to get rid of the evil by getting rid of this other through attack—behavioral, verbal, or thought (special hate).

This then comes down to a very simple practice: Watch yourself minute by minute, hour by hour, day by day, and learn to become aware of even the slightest discomfort. This then becomes your own call for help: "I am doing it again. I am making a decision in my mind to push love away. Rather than accept responsibility for it, I have projected it out onto the world where I can blame someone or something else for my discomfort." Such honesty with oneself is at the heart of the process of forgiveness, and the means by which we shall all come at last to end the ego's dream of separation and death.

CLOSING READING

"GOOD FRIDAY"

I would like to conclude by reading a poem of Helen Schucman's, but I want to say a few words about it first. Since we have been talking about death, the poem of Helen's that I will read begins with the statement, "There is no death." It is a Good Friday poem written around Easter. Actually, it became the first poem in a trilogy, followed several months later by "Easter" and "Holy Saturday."

This poem, as you will see, summarizes many of the themes we have been discussing. Since it was written at Easter time, there are the obvious holiday themes. The very end of the poem says, for example: "Today shall you be with Me in our home." The "Me," of course, is Jesus, and the line is a reference to the famous scene in Luke's gospel where Jesus is crucified between two thieves (Luke 23:39-43). As a character in the gospels, and in this story especially, Jesus has an ego, as do the "good thief" and "bad thief." Jesus chooses to reward one and punish the other. The "good thief" recognizes Jesus, and is therefore told: "This day you will be with me in Paradise." The other thief could have cared less who was next to him on the cross, and so he went to the other place. That is the source of the line in Helen's poem.

There is one other line to which I would like to call your attention. It is in the third stanza, where Jesus says: "What never was cannot be now." "What never was" is death; therefore death could not exist now. The phrase "*cannot be now*" is another of the lines taken from *Hamlet*. In fact, this was Helen's very favorite passage in all of Shakespeare, indeed in all of literature—not so much for the beauty of the language, but for the cleverness of the writing. This passage occurs near the end of the play, just before Hamlet is to duel Laertes, who, as I mentioned, is Ophelia's brother.

By this point Ophelia has drowned herself, after having gone mad as a result of Hamlet's verbal mistreatment. Claudius, king and Hamlet's uncle, has talked Laertes into dueling Hamlet to avenge his sister's death. Claudius' hidden agenda, however, is to dispose of Hamlet once and for all. He had already attempted this by arranging for Hamlet to be put on a ship to England where he was to be murdered by his friends, Rosencrantz and Guildenstern. Hamlet, however, discovered the plot in time, and when a pirate ship came along he jumped ship and sailed back to Denmark, where he then arranged to have the two traitors killed.

Horatio, Hamlet's trusted friend, warns him of the duel, saying that Hamlet is not in very good shape, while Laertes is. Hamlet's reply is that if he is going to die, then so be it:

> *Not a whit* [I am not concerned at all], *we defy augury* [providence]:
> *there's a special providence in the fall of a sparrow. If it be now,*
> *'tis not to come; if it be not to come, it will be now; if it be not now,*
> *yet it will come: the readiness is all.*   (V,ii,218)

Hamlet is saying that if death is going to happen now, it will not come in the future. If it is not going to come in the future, it will happen now. If it does not happen now, yet it will come. In other words, death is inevitable, and whenever it happens, it happens.

When Hamlet states *"the readiness is all,"* he means it is the readiness for death—one's *attitude* towards death—that is important. This idea of readiness, incidentally, is discussed in *A Course in Miracles* in both the text and manual, in the sense that readiness does not mean mastery (T-2.VII.7; M-4.IX.1:10). The meaning is that you do not have to master the Course in order to implement it in your life; you do not have to master forgiveness in order to be ready to learn it. In other words, you do not have to be perfect to study this Course. You need only be *willing*. In *A Course in Miracles*, therefore, *"readiness is all"* means that it is your *little willingness* to be taught how to forgive that is necessary, not your total commitment. In the context of *Hamlet*, the phrase reflects the inevitability of death, because Hamlet believed his guilt was real and therefore punishment inevitable. Thus Helen says with Jesus in the poem: "What never was cannot be now," meaning that death never was; an inherent illusion, it could never be, and thus forgiveness is complete.

I have been promising Helen for a long time I would discuss that line in Hamlet, so I have happily fulfilled my promise. We close now with this lovely poem:

Good Friday

There is no death. But there is quietness
Beyond the reaches of the world; a peace
Which only life can give. It is the life
That is the gift of God. All conflicts cease
Within this life. It beats in harmony
With all creation, beyond any sound
The world can hear. It sings a different song,
And where it reaches, there is holy ground.

There is no death. Whom God created whole
Is whole forever. Who can crucify
Eternal life? And who can bring to dust
Whom God has willed immortal? Can he die
Who rises past the universe, to rest
At one with his Creator? So are we
Ensured to Life. There is no death because
God's Son belongs to Immortality.

This is a day of joy. Today the world
Lays down its dreams beside a cross that was
Itself a dream. Behold the dream of death
And waken, seeing that it had no cause,
And so did not exist. What never was
Can not be now. Today we pass it by,
For this the purpose of this day should be:
What is made whole is whole, and cannot die.

Do not confuse the cross with sacrifice,
Nor death with life. The Will of God is one,
And knows no differences nor opposites.
In love it has created but one Son,
In whom the whole creation still remains.
How can his name be changed who bears the Name
His Father called as His? He does not change,
Because his will forever is the same.

What does he yearn for but his Father's house?
Had he a different will his death might be
Reality. But when he reconciled
What never had an opposite, then he
Could never die. His life is not his own,
Being of God. This day arise and come
With Me. For there is life. It is God's Will.
Today shall you be with Me in our home.

(The Gifts of God, pp. 106-107)

APPENDIX

"TO BE, OR NOT TO BE"

To be, or not to be: that is the question:
Whether 'tis nobler in the mind to suffer
The slings and arrows of outrageous fortune,
Or to take arms against a sea of troubles,
And by opposing end them. To die: to sleep;
No more; and by a sleep to say we end
The heart-ache, and the thousand natural shocks
That flesh is heir to, 'tis a consummation
Devoutly to be wish'd. To die, to sleep;
To sleep: perchance to dream: ay, there's the rub;
For in that sleep of death what dreams may come,
When we have shuffled off this mortal coil,
Must give us pause: there's the respect
That makes calamity of so long life;
For who would bear the whips and scorns of time,
The oppressor's wrong, the proud man's contumely,
The pangs of despised love, the law's delay,
The insolence of office, and the spurns
That patient merit of the unworthy takes,
When he himself might his quietus make
With a bare bodkin? who would fardels bear,
To grunt and sweat under a weary life,
But that the dread of something after death,
The undiscover'd country from whose bourn
No traveller returns, puzzles the will,
And makes us rather bear those ills we have
Than fly to others that we know not of?
Thus conscience does make cowards of us all,
And thus the native hue of resolution
Is sicklied o'er with the pale cast of thought,
And enterprises of great pitch and moment
With this regard their currents turn awry
And lose the name of action.

Hamlet (III,i,56)

INDEX OF REFERENCES TO *A COURSE IN MIRACLES*

text

workbook for students

manual for teachers

clarification of terms

The Song of Prayer

The Gifts of God